AGRICULTURAL POLICY AND SUSTAINABILITY:
Case Studies from India, Chile, the Philippines and the United States

Edited by Paul Faeth

WORLD RESOURCES INSTITUTE

September 1993

Kathleen Courrier
Publications Director

Brooks Belford
Marketing Manager

Hyacinth Billings
Production Manager

World Bank Photo by Tomas Sennett
Cover Photos

Contents

Acknowledgments

This report is the result of research conducted over several years with help from many people, and I am indebted to them all. I am especially grateful to Robert Repetto, whose vision inspired this research and whose intellectual and administrative counsel helped to keep it on track. Although they are no longer with WRI, I also wish to thank Mohamed El-Ashry and Gus Speth for the direction and insight they lent to this project in its formative stages.

Funding for the study was provided by The Rockefeller Foundation, The Joyce Foundation, The Ford Foundation, the United Nations Environment Programme, and the Wallace Genetic Foundation, Inc.

I wish to express my deep appreciation to several people who provided analytical assistance. In particular, Kim Kroll and Jim Reynolds (of the Rodale Institute's Research Center) provided simulation results for the methodological extension of the U.S. case studies, Gary Lesoing (of the University of Nebraska's Research Station at Meade) provided soil carbon data for the Nebraska case study, and Verel Benson and Jimmy Williams (of the Blacklands Agricultural Research Station at Temple, Texas) provided invaluable help with the EPIC model used in the Indian and U.S. case studies.

My special thanks go as well to WRI colleagues Ann Thrupp, Carrie Meyer, Walt Reid, Robert Blake, Robert Livernash, and Stephen Gasteyer, who read drafts and provided helpful comments. I am also grateful for the helpful comments provided by external reviewers Muhammad Akhtar, Gerald Carlson, Gunvant Desai, Sandra Postel, Vernon Ruttan, Sara Scherr, Scott Swinton, and V.S. Vyas.

I owe a unique debt of gratitude to Kathleen Lynch, who provided significant help editing successive drafts—and to Katy Perry for cheerfully handling what seemed like endless revisions of text and tables.

Finally, I owe thanks to Kathleen Courrier for editorial assistance, Hyacinth Billings for managing the production process, and Karen Holmes and Sheldon Cohen for help with the financial development of the project.

P.F.

Foreword

In many areas of the world, today's agriculture is unsustainable. The symptoms appear throughout the world's farming regions—salinization, erosion, soil compaction and waterlogging, water pollution and depletion, and desertification. Some 1.2 billion hectares of land—an area larger than India and China combined—have been seriously degraded since 1945. Hunger, already a daily reality for the world's poorest billion people, is growing. World population is expected to double again by mid-century. If current land degradation trends continue, one has to wonder how farmers will grow enough food for the more populous world of the next century.

Conventional economic analysis obscures the degradation of the natural resource base that supports agriculture. Changes in the productivity of natural resources simply are not taken into account. Until now, economic research on agriculture has failed to measure sustainability and to reveal how policies biased in favor of conventional farming methods may damage the resource base over the long term.

Consider the policy and research environment that favors agrochemical use in the United States, for instance. Land and labor are the most expensive production factors, while agrochemicals are cheap. For the past fifty years, agricultural research has focused on substituting what is cheap—chemicals—for what is expensive—land and labor. U.S. agricultural policy encourages this process by restricting land use. Heavy use of

agrochemicals can bring high yields in the short run, but the cumulative environmental damages can be considerable. In fact, farm run-off has become the single largest source of surface-water pollution in the United States, thanks partly to research and policy that have paid insufficient attention to natural resource degradation.

WRI has filled this research gap by using natural resource accounting methods to get a clearer picture of the relationship between farm policies and sustainability. How farm policies affect the production choices that farmers make—and how those choices affect environmental and human health—is the main question taken up in *Agricultural Policy and Sustainability: Case Studies from India, Chile, the Philippines, and the United States* by Senior Associate Paul Faeth and nine colleagues at WRI and elsewhere. By quantifying the environmental impacts of various combinations of cropping systems and farm policies, the authors demonstrate that farm policy is stacked against resource-conserving farming methods in all but one of the six areas studied. They found that the real costs of conventional farming methods are miscalculated in both the developing world and the United States. Like surface-water damage from farm run-off in Pennsylvania, for instance, groundwater depletion in the Punjab and pesticide-induced illness in the Philippines are ignored in calculating farm income, which would be much lower if these costs were included.

Three common themes emerged as the authors conducted these case studies. First, economic analysis that fails to measure changes in the productivity of natural resources will make farming practices that degrade the resource base look more valuable than those that conserve it. Second, when changes in the natural resource base *are* included in calculating farm income, resource-conserving production practices can compete economically and financially with conventional ones. And, finally, policies that encourage inappropriate natural resource use can cause significant economic and fiscal losses, as well as environmental ones.

To encourage the transition to resource-conserving agricultural methods that is in every nation's long-term interest, the authors recommend that governments reform their agricultural institutions and policies and improve the tools for monitoring and evaluating policy performance. Among their eight recommendations, three especially stand out:

- Governments should eliminate subsidies that encourage the degradation or depletion of natural resources—for instance, the electricity subsidies that lead to groundwater depletion in India and the pesticide subsidies that make unhealthy practices profitable in the Philippines.

- To reduce both fiscal costs and environmental damages, industrial countries should revise their farm income-support programs, tying support to need and to stewardship of the natural resource base, not to commodity production.

- Governments should revise the agricultural economic indicators reported in official statistics, making them reflect the depletion and degradation of natural resources. Assuming that the productivity of these resources is irrelevant to national economic health is especially misleading in the case of a resource-based sector such as agriculture.

Agricultural Policy and Sustainability augments the analyses set forth in *Paying the Farm Bill: U.S. Agricultural Policy and the Transition to Sustainable Agriculture*. The report should help economists analyze sustainability, policy-makers grapple with broad questions of societal well-being, farmers assess the sustainability of their operations, and citizens ensure that their tax dollars protect the agricultural resource base instead of encouraging its degradation. The policy changes recommended in both reports sometimes represent a vast departure from current policies—a measure of how much the political environment must evolve to promote sustainable agricultural systems. However, there is a growing awareness among farmers, researchers, conservationists, agricultural officials, and some manufacturers of agricultural chemicals that fundamental change is necessary. To further the policy dialogue, WRI researchers are now expanding their natural resource accounting framework to study U.S. agriculture as a whole, creating the database and analytical tools that policy-makers and farmers need to assess—and enhance—agricultural sustainability.

We would like to thank The Rockefeller Foundation, The Joyce Foundation, The Ford Foundation, the Wallace Genetic Foundation, Inc., and the United Nations Environment Programme, whose generous financial support made this study possible. To all, we are deeply grateful.

Jonathan Lash
President
World Resources Institute

I. Overview and Recommendations

Paul Faeth

Compelling physical evidence from around the world suggests that current farming practices in many areas cannot be sustained much longer. But since conventional economic indicators used in the agricultural sector do not include measures of environmental damage, and such evidence rarely makes its way into economic decisionmaking. Indeed, agricultural sustainability—though broadly recognized as important—is given little weight in economic policy-making. No commonly employed indicators measure it, no accepted conventions value it, and no widely accepted definition describes it. If agricultural sustainability is considered at all, it is an afterthought.

When agricultural sustainability is left out of economic policymaking, distortions that threaten sustainability look rational. Subsidies that encourage the inefficient use of inputs and resources, production practices that degrade resources, and income-support programs that restrict crop rotations, may all seem socially valuable. In fact, all entail large social costs. To keep these costs down, economic analysis must be redirected to promote agricultural sustainability, account for natural resource use, and reflect the true value of agricultural production and policy.

Growing competition for dwindling resources. As global population and income continue to grow, demand for food, fuel, fiber, and water increases. At the same time, the Earth's natural capital is declining. To keep up, agriculture must be put on a sustainable footing. Soil degradation from erosion, salinization, compaction, and depletion of organic matter have made an estimated 2 billion hectares of once-arable land irreversibly unproductive. An estimated 430 million hectares of arable land has been destroyed permanently by accelerated erosion alone—about 30 percent of the currently cultivated cropland (Lal and Pierce, 1991). Without conservation measures, over 500 million hectares of rainfed cropland may become unproductive over the long-term in Asia, Africa, and Latin America (World Commission on Environment and Development, 1989).

The off-farm environmental costs of farming may be even greater than soil-productivity losses. In the United States, for example, agricultural nutrients and sediments are by far the largest primary source of river and lake pollution (WRI, 1988). Annually, agricultural lands in the United States discharge 1.1 billion tons of suspended solids (water-borne particles), 500 million tons of dissolved soils, 1.2 million tons of phosphorous, and 4.7 million tons of total nitrogen (Lal and Pierce, 1991). Crops absorb at most 50 to 60 percent of the nitrogenous fertilizers applied to them, and much of the rest pollutes ground and surface waters (Lal and Pierce, 1991). As agriculture's share of the economy shrinks and competing demands for natural resources from nonagricultural sectors grow, the economic value of environmental damage from agriculture mounts.

A definitional quandary. Given the increasing awareness of the environmental problems associated with conventional agriculture, many researchers and organizations are struggling to define "sustainable agriculture." Almost every definition hinges on maintaining productivity and farm profitability while minimizing environmental impacts. However, none of these definitions has been quantitative, and the productivity of the natural resource base—fundamental to sustainability—has not yet been factored into definitions of agricultural productivity. The notion of agricultural sustainability has therefore been of only limited use to policy-makers and researchers attempting to determine the effects of various policies and technologies.

Broadly defined, sustainability means that economic activity should meet current needs without impinging on future options. In other words, the resources needed in the future must not be depleted to satisfy today's consumption (World Commission on Environment and Development, 1987). Textbook definitions of income take this notion of sustainability into account (Hicks, 1946; Edwards and Bell, 1961): income is defined as the maximum amount that can be consumed this year without reducing potential consumption in future years (without, that is, consuming capital assets).

Accounting systems for both businesses and nations include a capital consumption allowance. This cost, a yearly depreciation of capital, is subtracted from net revenues in calculating annual income. Like other forms of capital, the natural resource base provides a flow of economic benefits over time, but, historically, changes in its productivity have escaped accountants' notice. Changes in human-made capital are preeminent in accounting systems, implying that natural resource productivity is of negligible value in current production systems. Nations, businesses, and farmers account for the depreciation of assets, such as buildings and tractors, as they wear out or become obsolete, but ignore changes in the productive capacity of natural resources. As one accounting textbook put it: *With the exception of land,* * [tangible] assets gradually wear out or otherwise lose their usefulness with the passage of time..."(Niswonger and Fess, 1977)

_____
* Emphasis ours

Yet, a large body of evidence shows that the productivity of agricultural resources is anything but static. Erosion and salinization can have enormous impacts on the productivity of agricultural soils. Depletion and contamination can damage groundwater resources. The pollutants in agricultural runoff can severely reduce the productivity of ecosystems and drastically shorten a reservoir's life.

Current accounting practices simply don't capture the losses. Soil can be eroded, groundwater depleted or contaminated, wildlife poisoned, and reservoirs filled with sediment, but the losses have no apparent impact on agriculture's private or public value. No depreciation allowance is applied against current income for the degradation of these resources, even though the loss of asset productivity jeopardizes future income. Standard accounting practices thus misrepresent a decline in wealth as an increase in income.

Two reasons have been given for ignoring natural capital. One is that the scale of the human economy is small relative to the amount of natural capital. The other is that human-created capital is a near-perfect substitute for natural capital. But neither of these assumptions stands up in today's world. As for the first, the scale of the world economy is enormous and instances of resource degradation and depletion abound. As for the second, natural resources are more appropriately viewed as complements to human capital and not as direct substitutes (Daly and Cobb, 1989). Agricultural technology, for example, will perform much better on healthy soils, than on degraded ones.

Applying sustainability to agricultural economics. The main reason income is measured is "...to give people an indication of the amount which they can consume without impoverishing themselves...[T]he practical purpose of income is to serve as a guide for prudent conduct..."(Hicks, 1948) If the guide is somehow misleading, it follows that the conduct will be imprudent.

Conway (1986) defines sustainability as "the ability of a system to maintain its productivity

2

when subject to stress or perturbation." (A stress is a relatively small but regular disturbance, such as erosion or salinization whereas a perturbation is a relatively large and infrequent disturbance, such as drought.) According to basic accounting principles and Conway's definition, production systems that damage soil structure or deplete the soil of nutrients, organic matter or biota, are unsustainable.

If soil were depreciated like other assets, agronomic sustainability could be quantitatively determined. Production practices that degraded soil productivity would result in reduced yields and would, therefore, be *depreciated*. Conversely, practices that increased soil productivity would *appreciate*.

The same yardstick can be used to measure groundwater, watersheds, and even human health. If a production practice takes a resource beyond its ability to replenish itself, that use of the resource would be unsustainable. The mining of groundwater, the pollution of an ecosystem beyond its absorptive capacity, and the impairment of human health from the use of pesticides are, accordingly, unsustainable. All are forms of capital consumption and should be treated as such in accounting systems. Indeed, if changes in natural resource assets are ignored, resource degradation is encouraged, if not guaranteed.

A natural resource accounting framework The following example taken from Part V of this report shows how natural resource accounting methods can be applied. Tables I-1 and I-2 compare net farm income and net economic value per acre for a conventional corn-soybean rotation in Pennsylvania, with and without allowances for natural resource depreciation. Table I-1, column 1, shows a conventional financial analysis of net farm income. The gross operating margin—crop sales less variable production costs—is shown in the first row ($75). Because conventional analyses make no allowance for natural resource depletion, the gross margin and net farm operating income are the same. Government subsidies ($16) are added to obtain net income ($91).

Table I-1. Net Farm Income: Conventional vs Natural Resource Accounting ($/ac/yr)

Item	Conventional Accounting	Natural Resource Accounting
Gross Operating Margin	75	75
Less Soil Depreciation	—	24
Net Farm Operating Income	75	51
Plus Government Commodity Subsidy	16	16
Net Farm Income	91	67

When natural resource accounts are included, the gross operating margin is reduced by a soil-depreciation allowance ($24) to obtain net farm operating income ($51) *(Table I-1, column 2)*. The depreciation allowance is an estimate of the present value of future income losses due to the impact of crop production on soil quality. The same government payment is added to determine net farm income ($67).

To determine net economic value *(Table I-2, column 2)*, $49 is subtracted as an adjustment for the off-site costs of soil erosion (such as sedimentation, impacts on recreation and fisheries, and impacts on downstream water users). Net economic value also includes the on-site soil depreciation allowance, but excludes income support payments. Even though farmers do not bear the off-site costs directly, these are real economic costs attributable to agricultural production and, as such, should be considered in calculating net economic value to society. Subsidy payments, by contrast, are a transfer from taxpayers to farmers, not income generated by agricultural production, so they are excluded from calculations of net economic value. In this example, when these adjust-

Table I-2. Net Economic Value: Conventional vs. Natural Resource Accounting ($/ac/yr)

Item	Conventional Accounting	Natural Resource Accounting
Gross Operating Margin	75	75
Less Soil Depreciation	—	24
Net Farm Operating Income	75	51
Less Off-Site Costs of Soil Erosion	—	49
Net Economic Value	75	2

ments are made, a $91 profit under conventional financial accounting becomes only a $2 gain under more complete economic accounting.

Methodological Background

In this report, the results of four case studies from three developing countries—India, Chile, and the Philippines—are presented along with an extended analysis of two previously published case studies for the United States (Faeth et al., 1991). These studies grapple in economic terms with the slippery concept of agricultural sustainability. The aim here is to sketch in the shadowy outlines and to quantitatively reformulate the many qualitative definitions in use—and to provide both fodder for further economic analysis and broad directions for policy.

The analytical methods used in these case studies were designed to quantify the economic and environmental costs and benefits of a wide range of policy interventions. They were used to analyze the environmental costs of agricultural policies in both physical and monetary terms so that the benefits and costs of alternative policies could be compared.

The collection of studies relies on and advances the methods of natural resource accounting, which is a relatively simple way to arrive at quantitative measures of sustainability. Soil productivity, farm profitability, regional environmental impacts, and government fiscal costs can all be included within a natural resource accounting framework. In the six studies presented here, the authors compare profitability under alternative policy scenarios and the economics of conventional and alternative production systems when natural resources are accounted for.[1] These were critical omissions in past studies since the primary justification for sustainable agriculture will be overlooked if natural resource impacts are ignored. Additionally, any biases in current agricultural policy against certain types of practices, will also be reflected in the analysis, but may be undetected.

Each case study focusses on one or more significant impacts of an area's predominant production practices. To gauge potential improvement, alternative production practices that could help alleviate the problem are considered in each case. Supporting data for each case study are derived from earlier research in the study regions. In the U.S. and Philippine case studies, complete agronomic data and the information necessary to estimate crop budgets and important environmental impacts were either available from long-term field trials or could be generated from sophisticated analytical tools and data-collection methods. In the Chilean case study, the authors relied on impact data for a similar soil and climate in another setting and parametrically determined the point at which economic losses due to soil degradation would prompt a move to less damaging production systems. Research methods were adapted to suit each situation. Data sources, assumptions, and research methods for all the case studies are clearly laid out so that others seeking to improve upon these efforts will be able to do so.

Case Study Summaries

For all the studies, the overriding goal was to determine the inherent profitability of production practices in different agricultural settings, to gauge the extent of current biases and distortions of agricultural policy, and to point the way to policy alternatives that may encourage greater agricultural sustainability. The common thread was methodological: each study sought to quantify the principal environmental or health impacts of the study area's predominant cropping system.

India. The Indian case study focusses on alternatives to the conventional paddy-wheat production system in Ludhiana, one of twelve administrative districts in the Northwestern state of Punjab. This conventional paddy-wheat rotation requires heavy doses of inorganic fertilizers and pesticides, repeated deep plowing, and heavy use of groundwater. In this semi-arid region, more than 96 percent of the district is irrigated by tube-wells. Electricity subsidies encourage excessive water use, and groundwater tables are dropping about 0.8 meters a year. Water use is thus fundamentally unsustainable.

Eighteen combinations of tillage, irrigation, and fertilization practices were analyzed for paddy-wheat, the principal rotation, and three more for maize-wheat. Three levels of water use for the paddy-wheat rotation were tested: overuse, recommended use, and less than recommended use. The paddy-wheat rotation was also compared with conventional and conservation tillage. Both rotations were analyzed under three different soil-fertility management regimes: complete reliance on inorganic fertilizers, a mix of inorganic fertilizers and farmyard manure, and a mix of inorganic fertilizers and a green manure, *sesbania*.

In this study, financial and economic values for each farming practice were compared. By definition, the financial value—net farm income (NFI)—of a farming practice reflects current and future costs, including those of groundwater and soil depreciation, but ignores off-site environmental damage borne by others. In contrast, the economic value to society—net economic value (NEV)—includes one category of these off-site costs of sediment clean-up and removal, as well as on-site costs; comparing the two values revealed that resource-conserving farming practices are most profitable to farmers and most valuable to society.

Five policy options were tested. These policy scenarios are combinations of subsidized versus unsubsidized pricing regimes for fertilizers, electricity, and crops:

1. **Current policy**, as represented by subsidized prices for fertilizers and electricity for irrigation pumping, and procurement prices for commodities that are below world prices.

2. **Removing commodity support for consumers** and using the commodity's social value. Input prices remain unchanged.

3. **Removing input subsidies** using prices that reflect the cost of these inputs to society. Commodity prices are set below border prices, as under current policy.

4. **Removing commodity *and* input subsidies** and using social costs instead of input prices (excluding such externalities as groundwater pollution) and shadow prices for commodities.

5. **Free World Trade**, intended to represent a completely undistorted economic situation.

Figure I-1 shows the net farm income and net environmental costs for the predominant and two most profitable and resource-conserving alternative rice-wheat practices. For each, net farm income is given under four of the five policy scenarios tested. Under current policy, the predominant practice has a net farm income of 198,000 Rupees per hectare over thirty years. Accordingly, groundwater depreciation, soil depreciation, and off-site costs have a social value of 57,000 Rupees—more than a fourth of gross income. In contrast, the most

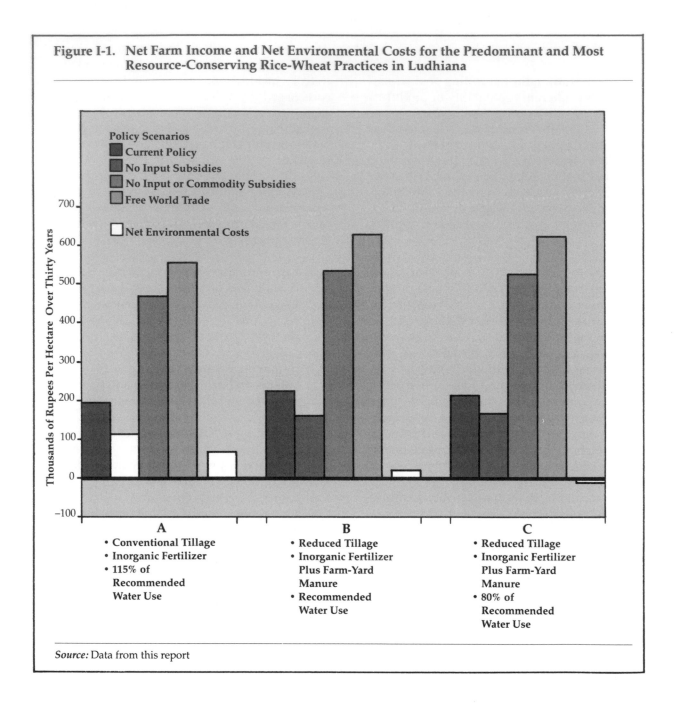

Figure I-1. Net Farm Income and Net Environmental Costs for the Predominant and Most Resource-Conserving Rice-Wheat Practices in Ludhiana

Policy Scenarios
- Current Policy
- No Input Subsidies
- No Input or Commodity Subsidies
- Free World Trade

Net Environmental Costs

Thousands of Rupees Per Hectare Over Thirty Years

A
- Conventional Tillage
- Inorganic Fertilizer
- 115% of Recommended Water Use

B
- Reduced Tillage
- Inorganic Fertilizer Plus Farm-Yard Manure
- Recommended Water Use

C
- Reduced Tillage
- Inorganic Fertilizer Plus Farm-Yard Manure
- 80% of Recommended Water Use

Source: Data from this report

resource-conserving practice (third group of Figure I-1) has a 9 percent higher net farm income and no net environmental costs.

Figure I-1 also shows that, though net farm income goes down when input subsidies are removed regardless of the practice, the impact is greatest for the predominant practice, which is the most dependent on subsidized inputs. When both input subsidies and consumer commodity support are removed, net income for each practice more than doubles. Implicitly, then, farmers are being taxed because commodity prices are being kept artificially low. Under free world trade, income would go up even more. Under each of these scenarios, profitability under a resource-conserving regime increases far more than under a resource-degrading regime.

Groundwater depletion is the most costly and seemingly inevitable effect of conventional production practices under paddy-wheat rotation in Ludhiana. The combination of porous soils and arid climate will inevitably make groundwater use unsustainable. Even at water use levels 20 percent below those recommended, groundwater may still decline significantly. Unless production practices are developed that dramatically reduce water use, any paddy production system may be unsustainable in this region.

The predominant rice-wheat farming system in Ludhiana is much more environmentally damaging, less profitable to farmers, and much less economically valuable to society than alternative farming systems that conserve natural resources. In fact, the net present value of groundwater depreciation calculated at subsidized electricity rates equals about 6 percent of gross operating margin. Consequently, the authors conclude, pricing reform, research on water management and alternative cropping systems, and better monitoring of the groundwater problem are all needed to put farming in Ludhiana on a more sustainable footing.

Chile. The Chilean study focusses simultaneously on the commercial and peasant production sectors for wheat. To give a more realistic picture of the value of agricultural production, estimates of soil productivity losses are included in net income calculations for production alternatives in both sectors. The inescapable conclusion is that farmers could face large financial losses if soil erosion from conventional and traditional production practices continues to cut yields.

More than 70 percent of all farms in Chile are smaller than 5 hectares. These peasant[2] (*campesino*) farms comprise less than 10 percent of all agricultural land. Most are located on marginal lands, and their productivity is low. Commercial farms, in contrast, while making up only 4 per-

cent of all farms, account for 44 percent of all land in production. On these farms, fertilizer and chemical use is heavy, access to irrigation is ample, and wheat yields are about three times those achieved on peasants' lands.

Conventional production practices on commercial farming were compared to organic alternatives, as were traditional practices for the peasant sector. Area under cultivation, soil depreciation, labor use, and sectoral net income are reported for eight economic scenarios. Off-site costs were not estimated, but the off-site damages per ton of eroded soil required to cause a shift in the economic value of the commercial cropping practices, were determined analytically.

In the eight scenarios, the three conventional and organic alternatives for commercial farming and the two traditional and three organic alternatives for peasant wheat production entail varying levels of input use. Labor and draft power are substituted for herbicides, and the combination of fertilizers and the amounts are also varied. Information on the commercial and organic alternatives was derived from short-term agronomic studies conducted at research centers in Chile. The various practices represent those used predominantly in central Chile and the experimental organic technologies available today.

The eight scenarios were run using a linear programming model. The model provides estimates of land allocation, the production of wheat, the corresponding production factors, soil depreciation, implicit wage rates for peasant farmers, labor demand, and total net income. The model simulates the choices that commercial and peasant farmers may make to maximize their net income. It then distributes land optimally across practices, according to crop sales, cost of production, soil depreciation, and production constraints (such as the availability of land or labor within the peasant family). A wide range of scenarios were tested, including alternative wage rates for labor, alternative prices for fertilizers and chemicals, a lower discount rate for peasants, and a higher wheat price (assuming a movement to world-wide free trade).

The results suggest that, under the current price structure, costs, and benefits of organic methods, peasant farmers have incentives to adopt organic practices. But organic practices have higher labor requirements and much lower yields in the commercial setting than on peasant farms, so commercial farmers do not have financial incentives to switch to organic technologies. The adoption of alternative farming practices appears to be limited by the availability of profitable alternatives in the commercial sector and by economic insecurity and limited extension efforts in the peasant sector.

The Philippines. Different pest-control strategies have different ecological and health impacts, depending on the type, amount, and schedule of application. The economics of four pest-control strategies for rice production in one region in the Philippines were examined in this case study to further understanding of the broader productivity impacts of pest control and pesticide use.

1. *complete protection*, requiring on average nine sprays, three each for the vegetative, reproductive, and ripening stages of crop growth, and sometimes two sprays during seedbed preparation;

2. the *economic threshold* method, requiring treatment only when a pre-set threshold for economic damage has been reached. Often, spraying is unnecessary and no more than two applications are required;

3. *natural control*, leaving pest control to the natural predator-prey dynamics of the paddy ecosystem. Management focuses on preserving or creating hospitable environments for predators through soil management and the selection of plant varieties and alternative host species; and

4. *farmers' practice* (or current local practice), spraying most commonly two or three times a season. Extremely hazardous chemicals are commonly used.

Through detailed physical and laboratory examinations of farmers in the study area and information on their pesticide-use practices, treatment costs were calculated to determine the cost of restoring individuals to health. When such health costs are ignored, farmers' practice and natural control appear to be the most economical methods, depending upon whether the season is wet or dry. Both practices have higher net benefits than either the economic threshold or complete protection practices. Input price changes have the greatest impact on relative benefits. Farmers using current practices or natural control reap the greatest benefits under a scenario of high pesticide prices coupled with a high output price.

When their own health costs are considered, however, natural control is always the best economic strategy for farmers. It has higher net benefits than the other treatments, including farmers' practice. Complete protection has 50 percent lower net benefits than the others. These results hold true under a variety of input and output-pricing alternatives.

Figure I-2 presents the net benefits and health costs of each of the four pest-management practices. The net benefits of farmers' practice and biocontrol, not including health costs, are almost identical, at about 14,000 pesos per hectare during the dry season. Health costs for farmers' practice total about 720 pesos per season, or about 5 percent of net benefits. Since biocontrol involves no pesticide use, there are no associated health costs. For the complete control practice, net benefits total 11,846 pesos per hectare per season. Health costs for this practice add up to about 7,500 pesos, or more than 60 percent of net benefits. If health costs were included, net benefits would drop to only 4,396 pesos. Even for the economic threshold practice, health costs equal more than 9 percent of net benefits.

Under normal circumstances, these results suggest, the natural pest-control option is often the most economical. Further, when pesticide-related health costs are accounted for, natural control has the greatest benefits, even for risk-averse farmers. For this reason, the authors suggest that

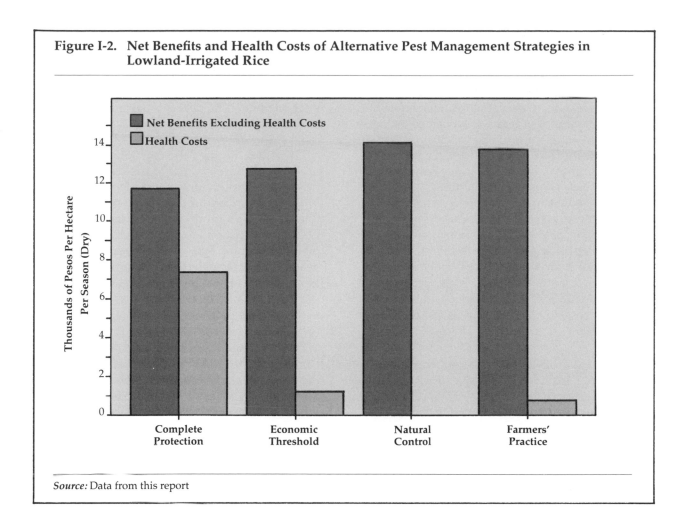

Figure I-2. Net Benefits and Health Costs of Alternative Pest Management Strategies in Lowland-Irrigated Rice

Source: Data from this report

alternative pest-management strategies should be developed in a broader health and ecological context. National pesticide policies should greatly restrict use of the most hazardous pesticides in rice production and eliminate all subsidies on pesticide use.

United States. Case studies in Pennsylvania and Nebraska compare commonly used conventional farming systems, which rely on heavy use of fertilizers and pesticides, with alternative systems, which rely on crop rotations and tillage practices for soil-fertility maintenance, moisture control, and pest management. In both case studies, five policy options were tested to determine their constraints on and incentives to farmers:

1. The 1985 basic commodity programs, and

2. The 1990 basic commodity programs;

3. The Integrated Farm Management (IFM) Program Option, intended to promote sustainable production practices;

4. The so-called Dunkel Test, a proposal put forward for discussion in a recent round of negotiations for the General Agreement on Tariffs and Trade (GATT); and

5. A fertilizer and pesticide input tax.

In these two studies, which update earlier research reported in *Paying the Farm Bill* (Faeth et al, 1991) estimates of environmental costs are based on detailed physical, agronomic, and economic modeling of soil, water, and chemical transport from the field and the implications of these processes for water quality and soil fertility, while physical estimates are extended to include soil carbon sequestration. The conclusions remain the same as for the earlier study: U.S. farm income support programs discourage resource-conservation. Base acreage constraints and commodity programs that cover only seven crops put resource-conserving crop rotations at a financial disadvantage, even though farming practices that reduce soil erosion and improve soil productivity greatly benefit society as a whole and the conventional subsidized practices can engender large net economic losses for the nation through soil erosion or damage to recreation areas, fisheries, and navigation.

Another conclusion is that recent changes in agricultural legislation have not provided the incentives necessary for sustainability, and administrative interpretations of the law have kept it from improving resource management as much as it could. Indeed, the basic incentive structure of U.S. farm programs works against sound resource management. Farmers are paid according to how much of the defined "program crops" they produce. Any practice that reduces the acreage of this small set of program crops reduces government support. In other words, farmers who plant non-program crops to control pests and manage soil fertility would receive less government support than farmers who participated in the programs but paid no heed to environmental impacts.

Figure I-3 shows the net economic values and government deficiency payments for the principal rotations in the Pennsylvania case study. Two aspects of these results are striking. First, under every policy scenario, the alternative practices have a much greater value to society than the conventional practices. Continuous corn in particular represents losses over a decade of more than $90 per acre per year under the current farm program. Yet, in spite of these economic losses, a farmer using this practice would receive more

than $50 per acre per year from the government. Second, for this case study, government payments decline as economic value goes up—the greater the economic value, the lower the government payment. The perverse nature of the current farm program is made clear in this Figure.

Two other findings also merit note. First, as passed by Congress, the IFM program appears to increase the profitability of practices that qualify for the program. As implemented by the USDA, however, the program would reduce profitability—an explanation for farmers' lack of interest in the IFM program. Second, because of the increased "flexibility" in the 1990 farm legislation, the Dunkel proposal would not require significant changes for U.S. policy, but would increase income for the practices tested here.

The challenge to agricultural policy-makers is to create incentives for farmers to adopt practices that are profitable, yet also in line with what is most economical for society. The research clearly indicates that direct income support programs should not be tied to commodity production but to financial need and environmentally sound management practices.

Common Themes

Several important themes emerged from an analysis of the case studies.

1. Economic analysis that excludes the value of productivity changes of natural resources or externalities will overstate the value of resource-degrading practices and understate the value of resource-conserving practices. This premise holds true for every case study examined here. For some instances, such as groundwater depletion in the Punjab, health costs in the Philippines, and surfacewater damage from erosion in Pennsylvania, these costs make up a large part of gross operating margin. Further, the costs of resource-degrading practices can make even the net economic value of financially profitable practices negative. Conversely, if benefits and costs are recognized, resource-conserving practices can, by generating significant benefits or

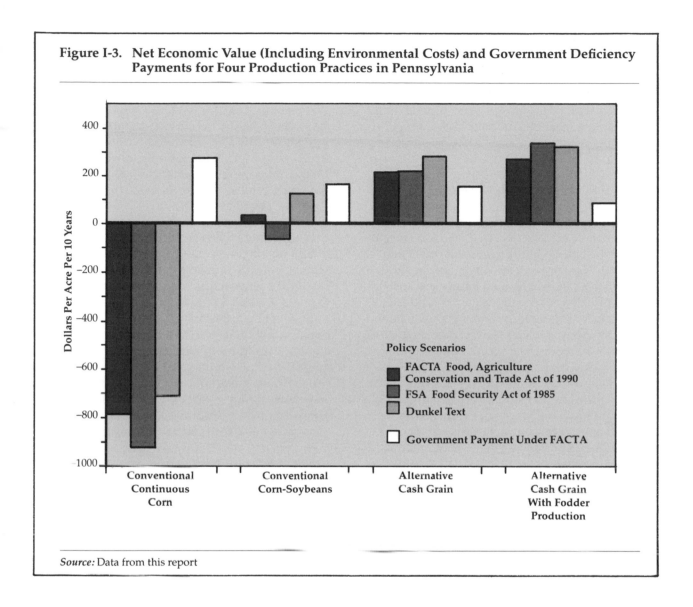

Figure I-3. Net Economic Value (Including Environmental Costs) and Government Deficiency Payments for Four Production Practices in Pennsylvania

Policy Scenarios

- **FACTA** Food, Agriculture Conservation and Trade Act of 1990
- **FSA** Food Security Act of 1985
- **Dunkel Text**
- **Government Payment Under FACTA**

Source: Data from this report

avoiding large costs, become the preferred option from both private and public viewpoints.

2. Resource-conserving production practices can compete economically and financially with conventional practices. When a more accurate picture of agricultural productivity is presented by including resource costs and benefits, production practices that conserve or enhance natural assets are economically as good as or better than the predominant practices. Five of the six case studies demonstrate this conclusion. (Commercial

production in Chile is the exception.) In four cases, a production practice that reduced resource degradation proved financially and economically superior to conventional practices. In one (Nebraska), a resource-conserving alternative was found to be competitive within a percentage point or two of the dominant system.

3. Policies that disregard the productivity of natural resource use in agriculture can diminish sustainability and cause significant economic and fiscal losses. The Indian, Philippine, and both U.S. case studies demonstrate this point. In the Punjab, large subsidies for electricity encourage the gross overuse of groundwater. In the Philippines, regulations ignore the health costs associated with hazardous insecticides and, in the United States, farm income subsidies are highest for farmers who use the most resource-degrading practices.

In each instance, official policies work against sustainability. They encourage production practices that have lower net economic value than resource-conserving practices and increase the subsidies and clean-up burden on taxpayers. Each case study also showed, however, how agricultural policies can be reformed to increase sustainability, improve net economic gain, and reduce fiscal outlays. This synergy is not possible, however, unless these policies reflect sound resource economics. Nor can the impact of policy on resource productivity be known unless the productivity of natural assets is explicitly accounted for. Excluding the cost of resource degradation from agricultural accounts does not eliminate the degradation and can prompt decision-makers to adopt poor policies and farmers, poor practices.

Recommendations

The case studies presented here support eight recommendations that would encourage sustainable agriculture and economic development. These recommendations cover institutional reform, policy reform, and the improvement of tools for monitoring and evaluating policy performance.

Policy Reform

Recommendation 1. **Subsidies that encourage natural resource degradation or depletion in any country should be eliminated.**

Public policy-makers are responsible for protecting the public welfare, including the natural resource base. But, resource and input subsidies lead to inefficient use—the antithesis of environmental sustainability. The Indian case study presented here shows how electricity subsidies lead

to the overexploitation of groundwater, and the Philippine study demonstrates how pesticide subsidies could make unhealthy practices profitable.

Agricultural production should be made subject to the "polluter pays" principle. Off-site damage from agriculture could be reduced if farmers were forced to pay for cleaning up their own pollution. Taxing or banning the most dangerous pesticides and cutting out subsidies on their use would be a good first step.

In the United States, agricultural polluters should no longer receive special treatment. Mining, construction, and other industries must pay local fines and fees for their off-site pollution. Farmers should be required to do the same. National or state pesticide and fertilizer taxes based on a sliding scale tied to environmental damage, would motivate farmers to use these inputs efficiently, helping to minimize ground- and surface-water pollution. *These tax revenues should be earmarked for agricultural research to help farmers reduce their reliance on pesticides and fertilizers.* (Several states already have such programs.)

Recommendation 2. **Industrial countries should eliminate agricultural support programs that distort economic signals to farmers and thus create commodity surpluses that entail heavy fiscal costs and excessive environmental damage.**

The industrial countries could contribute to agricultural sustainability worldwide by restructuring their own agricultural and trade policies. Their current policies support agricultural incomes at very heavy fiscal and environmental costs and induce the serious misallocation of agricultural resources worldwide. The structure of agricultural policy in industrial countries makes fiscal investment in farm income support a bad buy. These policy distortions hurt economic development at home and abroad, especially in the poorer countries, by lowering world commodity prices and restricting access to markets.

Farm income support programs should be tied to need and to the provision of environmental services, not to commodity production. Production practices that damage the environment should not receive public support. Program payments should be contingent upon the adoption of practices that rely principally on biological management of soil and pests, conserve the resource base, and enhance environmental productivity. Farm income should be temporarily subsidized during the conversion period. Available funds should be given only to farmers who really need help, as determined through means tests, and payment limitations should apply.

International agreements, such as the General Agreement on Tariffs and Trade, should continue to move toward the reduction or elimination of trade barriers and production subsidies. Each of the six case studies presented here included a scenario that mimics the opening of global markets. In every case, farmer profits increased, and in several cases sustainability was enhanced as the net income of resource-conserving practices improved. The U.S. case studies showed that taxpayers, farmers, and consumers all lose under the convoluted policies now in force. Policies that decouple production decisions from income support could continue to cushion the farm sector, but at reduced fiscal and environmental costs. Decoupling should in no way affect the maintenance or strengthening of appropriate phyto-sanitary standards.

Studies similar to those presented here should be conducted in the European Community and Japan to determine the environmental impacts and net economic value of their farm support programs. Such research would most likely show that large economic gains are possible if agricultural policies were reformed.

Institutional Reform

Recommendation 3. **Decisions on public funding for research should explicitly take into account the environmental costs and benefits of the research proposed.**

The scope, pace, and direction of agricultural research are key determinants of the adoption rate for agricultural technologies and of growth in agricultural productivity. Agricultural research

has often been driven by the relative prices or scarcity of land, labor, capital, and other production factors. Since World War II, labor and particularly land have become more expensive, sometimes as a result of physical constraints (as in Asia) and sometimes as a result of artificial controls on supply (as in the United States). At the same time, fertilizers, pesticides, and other production inputs have become relatively less expensive. Environmental services (the absorption of agricultural run-off, by-products, and waste, for instance) have been unlimited and unpriced—free to any agricultural producer at any level of disposal.

As a result, agricultural production has become input-intensive. Soil and pest-management strategies have focused on chemical rather than biological control methods, and environmental damage from agriculture has increased greatly.

Meanwhile, the criteria for evaluating the costs and benefits of publicly sponsored agricultural research programs have been seriously flawed, and the economic value of their impacts on natural resources systematically ignored. Government research funds have supported conventional farming systems, often to the detriment of alternatives. An about-face is needed.

Publicly funded research should place a much greater emphasis on conserving natural resources and minimizing the side effects of agriculture. *In cost/benefit analyses of agricultural research, a broadened definition of agricultural productivity must be used—one that includes the environmental costs and benefits.* Such analysis would show the greater social benefit of using technologies that conserve the environment.

Recommendation 4: **Research into sustainable farming practices should be given much higher priority and correspondingly higher funding.**

Economic studies have demonstrated that conventional agricultural research has been underfunded considering the benefits that it brings. In view of agricultural production problems in the developing countries and the environmental problems it spawns globally, much more money is justified for research in how to make agricultural production more sustainable.

In the international arena, the Consultative Group for International Agricultural Research (CGIAR) is the most prominent agricultural research institution. Its centers have produced many important new technologies, generally focused on individual crops. A number of CGIAR centers have developed new research programs and taken new directions focused on sustainability. But while CGIAR's responsibilities have been increasing, research funds in real terms have been declining. As CGIAR centers continue their important work and place new emphasis on natural resource management, their research will be increasingly difficult and costly. *Significant new funding should be made available from multilateral and bilateral aid institutions to support CGIAR's work on sustainable farming practices.*

In the United States, the Sustainable Agriculture Research and Education Program (formerly the LISA Program) is the only research program that supports the development of sustainable farming systems. Controversial since its inception, however, this program has never been adequately funded. Of the $40 million a year authorized in the 1990 Farm Bill, appropriations have never exceeded $7 million annually. *The USDA should request, and the Congress should appropriate, full funding for the Sustainable Agriculture Research and Education Program.*

Recommendation 5: **The CGIAR centers should work closely with farmers and nongovernmental organizations on research and extension.**

CGIAR research results have been disseminated through national agricultural research systems (NARSs) to extension programs and, finally, to farmers. This diffusion model has often broken down, however, due to funding shortfalls, lack of trained staff, or institutional weaknesses. In some cases, information may take too long to arrive or may not reach farmers at all, and CGIAR centers may need more feedback from farmers to gauge the usefulness of their work.

Private voluntary or nongovernmental organizations (NGOs) bridge this information gap more efficiently and less expensively than government can in many countries. Often, NGOs work directly with farmers to develop and promote appropriate agricultural technologies. For these reasons, more CGIAR centers should develop mutually beneficial partnerships with NGOs.

At the same time, farmers and NGOs should be more broadly represented on the boards of research institutions. The additional sensitivities and perspectives they would bring could benefit the research process and broaden political support for institutional research in industrial and developing countries alike.

Recommendation 6. **Multilateral development agencies should adopt natural resource accounting methods for agricultural project analysis.**

Billions of dollars in loans and grants for agricultural development are made every year by the World Bank, regional development banks, and bilateral development agencies. These loans make up a large part of agricultural investment in developing countries and have supported some of the biggest development pushes to date. Yet, none of the economic analysis behind this lending explicitly accounts for a project's use of natural resources.

The institutions that support these projects have come under heavy and frequent criticism for the environmental damage such investments entrain. That the damage was not intended or even foreseen points to the shortcomings of conventional economic analysis. Certainly, the development institutions already possess the talent and resources needed to do economic analysis in support of agricultural sustainability—the depreciation of natural assets, as is now done for man-made assets and the economic valuation of environmental externalities caused by agricultural production. *Natural resource accounting methods should become standard practice in project evaluation at international development institutions.*

Evaluation and Monitoring

Recommendation 7. **Physical monitoring of agriculture's environmental impacts should be drastically improved in developing countries.**

The foundation of any analysis of agricultural sustainability must rest on data that describe the physical environment and the physical impacts of alternative production choices. Yet, as the case studies demonstrate, this most basic information is often lacking, and existing data are often incomplete in temporal or geographic coverage. To fill this gap, agricultural resource surveys should be made periodically by state agencies to draw baselines for the main agricultural resources— soil and water.

International organizations such as the United Nations Environment Programme (UNEP) and the Food and Agriculture Organization (FAO) should develop simple, inexpensive, standardized data-collection techniques and analytical tools for use in developing countries and support the training necessary to use them.

Recommendation 8. **National economic indicators of the agricultural sector reported in official statistics and policy analyses should reflect the depletion and degradation of natural resources.**

Current methods for determining national and sectoral income can be terribly misleading indicators of sustainable economic development. By design, national income accounts ignore natural assets, assuming that the productivity of these resources is irrelevant to national economic health. Nothing could be farther from the truth, especially for nations and economic sectors such as agriculture that depend on natural resources.

The few studies comparing conventional and natural resource accounting methods of calculating national income show consistently that what has been counted as income actually amounts to losses in the form of natural resource depletion and degradation. Because resource depletion is really a form of capital consumption, conventional accounting methods overstate income and

skew economic planning. Not until the depreciation of natural assets is treated with the same seriousness as the depreciation of man-made assets will policy-makers and the public get the facts, and until then sustainability will remain a pipedream.

There may once have been a time in world economic development when natural resources were so abundant, and other economic priorities so pressing, that the condition of natural resources could be ignored without serious consequences. That time is long gone. Yet, although many resource and agricultural economists deal very credibly with natural resource and environmental issues, the environment is still routinely "assumed away" in national policymaking and economic modeling. By putting the environment outside the scope of macroeconomic and sectoral economic analysis, economists can mislead policy-makers and the public.

In the United States, appraisals of natural resource use and economic policy by the USDA's Economic Research Service (ERS) and Soil Conservation Service (SCS) should account for agricultural sustainability—explicitly and in economic terms. *ERS should adapt its policy models to include the depletion and depreciation of natural resources. SCS should develop natural resource accounts for U.S. agriculture in its next assessment under the Soil and Water Conservation Act, due in 1997. In addition, the United States Department of Commerce should accelerate its fledgling effort to develop natural resource accounts for the U.S. economy.*

This report should be considered a first effort in this regard. The hope is that others build on and improve it and that economic analysis of agricultural sustainability will soon be accepted as standard practice.

Notes

1. *See* for example: GRC Economics 1990; Knutson, et al, 1990; Tweeten and Helmers, 1990; Dobbs, Leddy, and Smolik, 1988; Goldstein and Young, 1987; Cacek and

Langner, 1986; Domanico, Madden, and Partenheimer, 1986; Helmers, Langemeier, and Atwood, 1986; Lockeretz et al., 1984.

2. The literal translation of the term *campesino* from Spanish is "peasant," which means nothing other than "small farmer." Anthropologists regularly use "peasant" in this context. Unfortunately, in English usage the word "peasant" sometimes carries a pejorative meaning. We use the term in this text in its academic sense, as it is the most appropriate term to define the farming systems under consideration.

II. Rice-Wheat Production in Northwest India

R.P.S. Malik and Paul Faeth

Conservation is good business. Of 20 alternative production practices tested in this case study, only two were less profitable than the most commonly used system for rice-wheat farming, and none caused greater environmental damage. The practical implications of this finding are immediate and alarming for India—the world's second most populous country. If it is to grow enough food for its 1.5 billion people in 2025 (WRR, 1992), productivity on the land now being farmed will have to continue to increase since no more arable land is available.

Background

Northwest India, particularly the Punjab, has been called "the granary of India." Over the past 30 years, the state has become the country's most agriculturally advanced region and the largest foodgrain supplier to government stocks. The rest of the Punjabi economy has also fared well.[1]

Agricultural growth in the Punjab has come mainly from institutional support and technological innovation. High-yielding plant varieties and external inputs such as fertilizers and pesticides have been introduced, and infrastructure (irrigation, rural electrification, roads) has been developed. Institutional support has come in the form of credit, research and extension, and pricing. Encouraged by a favorable price structure, rice production has taken off in this semiarid land. So many private tubewells have been drilled and groundwater is being depleted so fast that the long-term viability of rice production in the Punjab is now questionable.

There are two principal crop seasons in the Punjab. The wet summer season, *kharif*, is dominated by paddy, maize, cotton, and groundnut production. The predominant crops of the *rabi*, the drier winter season, are wheat and barley. Paddy production has surged from just 3 percent of gross cropped area in 1975 to about 32 percent currently. With this shift, maize, cotton, and groundnut production has declined drastically. Together, paddy and wheat account for almost 70 percent of the gross cropped area (Government of Punjab, 1990).

Agricultural production has become more intensive with the increase in paddy production and the advent of high-yielding varieties. Fertilizer consumption per hectare of gross cropped area soared to 227 kilograms in 1988–89 from 80 kilograms in 1975–76 (FAI, 1990). The number of crops per year and irrigation applications have also increased.

Study Focus

This case study focusses on Ludhiana, one of the Punjab's 12 administrative districts. The conventional paddy-wheat rotation in Ludhiana relies on heavy doses of inorganic fertilizers and pesticides, repeated deep plowing, and heavy use of groundwater. In this semiarid region, the

17

annual precipitation averages less than 700 millimeters, most of it falling between July and September. More than 96 percent of the district is irrigated by tubewells. Electricity subsidies encourage excessive water use. Available evidence suggests that farmers are currently irrigating paddy by about 15 percent over the recommended level. (Jain et al., 1989; Prihar and Grewal, 1988; Singh, 1987) As a result of over-irrigation and the large scale of rice production, groundwater tables are dropping about 0.8 meters a year. This particular area is not subject to significant salinization problems.

Eighteen combinations of tillage, irrigation, and fertilization practices were analyzed for the principal rotation, paddy-wheat, and three more for maize-wheat. No information was available for other rotations, including pulses. Three levels of water use for the paddy-wheat rotation were tested: 1. irrigation at current levels (15 percent over recommended levels); 2. recommended levels; and 3. 20 percent below the recommended level. Yield is the same for the first two levels of irrigation; yield declines by 8 percent under the third (PAU, 1987).

The paddy-wheat rotation was also compared with conventional and conservation tillage. Both rotations were analyzed with three different fertilization strategies: 1. complete reliance on inorganic fertilizers; 2. a mix of inorganic fertilizers and farmyard manure; and 3. a mix of inorganic fertilizers and a green manure, *sesbania*.

Financial and economic values for each farming practice were compared under five policy options over a 30-year production period. We define the financial value—net farm income (NFI)—of a farming practice to take into account current and future sales and costs, including groundwater and soil depreciation, but to ignore off-site environmental damage borne by others. NFI represents the value to the farmer. In contrast, the economic value to society—net economic value (NEV)—includes one category of these off-site costs of sediment cleanup and removal, as well as on-site costs. Under each of these economic scenarios, resource-conserving farming practices are

most profitable to farmers and most valuable to society. Current pricing practices in the Punjab, however, discourage conservation and long-term agricultural sustainability.

Environmental costs were estimated for each farming practice under each policy option in a natural resource accounting framework (after Faeth et al., 1991) to work out more complete measures of farm economics and agricultural productivity.

The alternative policy options analyzed were:

- **Current policy (CP)**, as represented by subsidized prices for fertilizers and electricity for irrigation pumping, and support/procurement prices for commodities.

- **Removal of commodity support (RCS) for consumers** and replacement by the commodity's shadow prices (border prices plus the difference in transportation costs). Input prices remain unchanged.

- **Removal of input subsidies (RIS)** and replacement by prices that reflect the cost of these inputs to society. Commodity prices as in current policy.

- **Removal of commodity and input subsidies (RCIS)** and replacement of government-set input prices by their value (not including externalities, i.e. groundwater pollution) and shadow prices for commodities.

- **Free World Trade (FWT)**, intended to represent a completely undistorted economic situation. In this scenario, input subsidies are removed. Commodity prices are derived from a simulation using the assumption that both the industrial and developing market economies liberalize their domestic agricultural and trade policies.

The prices of inputs and outputs under each policy option analyzed are presented in Table II-1. Shadow prices, used for the subsidy removal and free world trade scenarios, are derived in Annex Table AII-1. *(See Technical Annex.)*

Table II-1. Input and Output Prices

Policy Option	Input Prices			Output Prices		
	Nitrogen (Rs/kg)	Phosphorous (Rs/kg)	Electricity (Rs/kwh)	Rice (Rs/t)	Maize (Rs/t)	Wheat (Rs/t)
CP	6.65	7.57	0.15	3,800	2,800	2,730
RCS	6.65	7.57	0.15	7,539[a]	6,395	5,418
RIS	16.10	16.50	1.03	3,800	2,800	2,730
RCIS	16.10	16.50	1.03	7,539	6,395	5,418
FWT	16.10	16.50	1.03	8,454	7,263	6,196

CP = Current Policy; RCS = Removal of Commodity Support; RIS = Removal of Input Subsidies; RCIS = Removal of Commodity and Input Subsidies; and FWT = Free World Trade
a. The effective level of commodity support is equal to the output price under the RCS scenario minus the output price under the CP scenario.

Derivation of Natural Resource Accounts

The natural resource impacts of each production practice were analyzed by estimating allowances for groundwater and soil depreciation and off-site costs of dredging and hauling sedimentation from irrigation canals.

Groundwater depletion is the most costly and seemingly inevitable effect of conventional production practices under paddy-wheat rotation in Ludhiana. Paddy rice needs a great deal of water, and Ludhiana gets little rain and has porous soils. Even at water-use levels 20 percent below those recommended, groundwater may still decline about one-half meter per year. Thus, any paddy production system may be unsustainable in this region. The maize-wheat production system, in contrast, does not appear to deplete groundwater.

Groundwater Depreciation

A groundwater balance estimating method developed by the Directorate of Water Resources, Government of Punjab, was used to estimate annual incremental drops in groundwater for each of the three irrigation management systems. Based on these rates of decline, a schedule was determined for upgrading pumping motors and deepening bores. The faster that groundwater tables drop, the sooner motors must be replaced and bores deepened so water can be pumped from a greater depth. These accelerated depreciation rates are compared with normal depreciation schedules based on constant groundwater depth, and the accelerated costs are applied to the financial and economic analysis of each production practice as a groundwater depreciation allowance.

To estimate the state of groundwater resources in the Punjab, the Water Resources Directorate has compiled "blockwise"[2] statistics on annual recharge, draft, and groundwater balance for each district.[3] According to these data, Ludhiana's watertable declined in each year covered. (*See Table II-2 and Technical Annex.*)

Groundwater balances under each irrigation practice and rotation are shown in Table II-3. The rice-wheat rotations (first three columns) show consistent groundwater declines. Recommended water use levels for rice could help slow groundwater depletion by about 21 percent, but this still means a 20-meter decline over the 30-year period. A further 20-percent decrease in water application for rice would cut groundwater decline by 41 percent, with a 15-meter drop over 30 years. Based on the estimated rates of watertable decline, pumping capacity would have to triple over the 30-year time period of this study. Only

19

Table II-2. Estimated Changes in Watertable,[a] (Ludhiana District)

Year	Annual Recharge (ha-m)	Annual Draft (ha-m)	Water Balance (ha-m)	Change in Watertable (m)
1984	140,093	187,504	-47,411	-0.83
1988	135,089	204,588	-69,499	-1.22
1989	141,543	197,531	-55,988	-0.98

a. Change in Water Table = Water Balance/(Geographical Area * Specific Yield), where Specific Yield = 0.15, and Geographical Area = 379,000 hectares.

the maize-wheat rotation (not shown) eliminates groundwater depletion.

Under the rice-wheat rotation at 15-percent over-irrigation, a typical farm's operating costs would triple over 25 years owing largely to the need for progressively larger pumps.[4] *(See Table II-4.)* Under the other irrigation scenarios, the only essential difference is that the switch to a higher capacity pump and deeper bore occurs later.[5]

Groundwater depreciation costs were calculated as the difference in present value of capital and operating costs without any water-table decline and with the water-table decline under the option considered. For the base scenario (no water-table decline), pump size and operating costs remain constant and motors are replaced every 10 years. Figure II-1 shows the large future costs that farmers will face as groundwater is depleted.

Soil Depreciation

Soil erosion and long-term soil productivity are much less problematic than groundwater depletion in the study area. Crop prices assumed for the various policy scenarios were used to estimate the present value of yield changes. These values were then applied against each cropping practice's gross operating margin.

Soil erosion The estimated soil erosion rates are low. Over 30 years, wheat yields decline as much as 5 percent, but with offsetting gains in rice yields of up to 10 percent. For the paddy-wheat production systems, a combination of inorganic fertilizers, farmyard manuring, and reduced tillage improves rice yields the most and reduces wheat yields the least. For the wheat-maize systems, yields increase over time for the combinations of inorganic fertilizers and farmyard or green manure, but wheat yields decline under the system using only inorganic fertilizers.

Soil productivity Long-term soil productivity depends on the change in yields, the commodity prices, and the relative prices between crops. *(See Table II-5 and Technical Annex.)* For the cropping practices using inorganic fertilizers alone or in combination with green manure, the present value of the loss of wheat yield is greater than the gain in rice, or maize (in the case of inorganic fertilization).

Off-site costs of soil erosion Because erosion rates are low and the costs to correct damage are relatively low, off-site impacts from soil erosion are relatively small. *(See Table II-5 and Technical Annex.)* The cost of removing 100 m³ of sediment from water channels and throwing it on the banks of canals (locally known as *kassi* work) was set at Rs 525 by the Punjabi Directorate of Water Resources (September 1990). This cost converts to Rs 3.28 per ton of sediment.

Table II-3. Estimation of Changes in Groundwater Balance with Changes in Irrigation Water Use on Rice—1984 (Ludhiana District)

A. Net Current Groundwater Draft — 188 (000 ham)
  (i) For Rice (60%) — 113
  (ii) For Wheat and Other Crops (40%) — 75

B. Net Current Annual Recharge — 140 (000 ham)

	Water Use Level (% of recommended)		
	115	100	80
Draft			
1. Water Applied to Rice (meters/ha)			
–Crop Growth	2.40	2.08	1.68
–Nursery and Pre sowing	0.36	0.36	2.44
–Total	2.76	2.44	2.04
2. Estimated Groundwater Draft (000 ham) for Rice (pro rata basis)	113	99	83
3. Total Estimated Draft for all Crops (000 ham) (A(ii)+2)	188	174	158
Recharge[a]			
4. Reduction in Groundwater (000 ham) Applied to Rice (A(i)-2)	0	13	29
5. Reduction in Recharge to Groundwater (000 ham) as a Result of Lower Water Use on Rice	0	4.5	10
6. Estimated Annual Recharge[b] (000 ham) (B-5)	140	136	130
Groundwater Balance			
7. Estimated Groundwater Balance (000 ham)	-47	-39	-28
8. Estimated Decline in Water Table[c,d] (meters/yr)	0.8	0.7	0.5

Note: ham = hectare-meters (10,000 cubic meters)

a. Calculated by multiplying the new water application by the old groundwater draft for rice, and dividing by the old water application for rice and subtracting from the original. For the recommended water use, new groundwater draft is 112 - [(2.44 * 112)/2.76] = 13.

b. New groundwater recharge is the current recharge minus 35 percent of new total water application.

c. The annual water table decline is the groundwater balance divided by the specific yield (0.15) times the area (379,000 ha). For recommended water use annual water table change is -37000/(0.15 * 379,000) = -0.65.

d. Current water table level is -8 meters.

Numbers may not add due to rounding.

Table II-4. Typical Farm's Capital and Operating Costs for Irrigation Practice Using 115 Percent of Recommended Water Use
(Rs/3 ha over 30 yrs.)

Year	Depth to Water-table(m)	Engine BHP	Pumping Equipment & Accessories	Bore Deepening	Annual Operating Cost
0	8.00	10	11,220		1,678
6	12.80	15	16,060		2,482
12	17.60	20	20,790		3,281
18	22.40	25	26,400		4,121
21	24.80			10,000	
25	28.00	30	31,460		5,030

BHP = brake horsepower.

a. The cost of accessories in the total cost of pumping equipment and accessories is 10 percent of the cost of pumping equipment.
b. Annual operating expenses include expenses on repairs and maintenance and on electricity.
c. Cost of electricity has been taken at Rs 0.15 per kwh.
d. Repair and maintenance costs have been calculated at 5 percent of the cost of pumping equipment.

Assuming an average distance of 10 kilometers to agricultural fields for dumping, the cost of loading, transporting, and unloading comes to Rs 40 per ton of sediment. Added to the cost of dredging, the total cost of canal maintenance is about Rs 43 per ton of eroded soil.[6]

Policy Analysis

Net Financial Value. Our policy analysis revealed large differences in the net financial value of the various farming systems. These results clearly show that agricultural policy can dramatically affect the relative profitability of production practices. *(See Table II-6.)*

Under *current policy*, after accounting for soil depreciation and groundwater depletion costs, the largest financial returns are obtained by farming systems that reduce water consumption to recommended levels, reduce tillage operations, and use inorganic fertilizer alone or combined with farmyard manure. In contrast, the system used by most farmers in the region entails financial returns almost 20 percent lower. This difference is accounted for by the lower production costs and soil-depreciation allowance for reduced tillage and the lower groundwater user costs under the recommended water-use option.

Removing all consumer commodity support would double the net financial values of every production practice considered. The prices farmers currently receive for their crops are well below world market prices. Basically, producers pay a large implicit tax on rice, wheat, and maize. The relative positions of each production practice would change little, except that the systems using farmyard manure would be slightly more profitable.

Leaving commodity price subsidies intact but *removing producer input subsidies* would bring

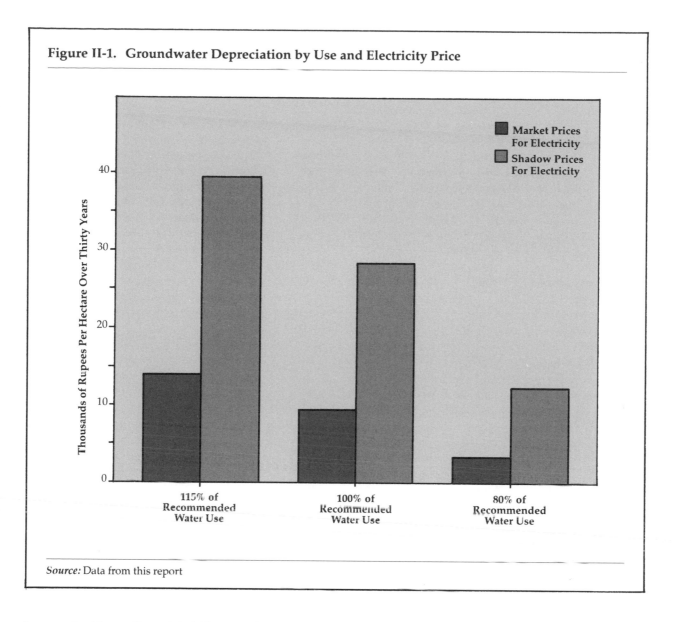

Figure II-1. Groundwater Depreciation by Use and Electricity Price

Source: Data from this report

about a significant financial shift toward the most resource-conserving production practices, widening the gap between these best practices and the worst. For the rice-wheat systems employing reduced tillage, the most profitable practice would use 20 percent less irrigation than recommended and a combination of farmyard manures and inorganic fertilizer.

Net financial value would drop for all practices, but the practices associated with the greatest groundwater depletion would lose the most

value. Because electricity prices, and therefore irrigation costs, would increase sharply, groundwater user costs would nearly triple for current water-use practices.

Removing both commodity support and input subsidies would also encourage the conservation of natural resources. The most resource-conserving rice-wheat system is 20 percent more profitable than the typical system using conventional tillage, overirrigating, and using only inorganic fertilizers. Due to higher crop prices, profitability

23

Table II-5. Soil Erosion, Crop Yields, and Off-Site Costs

Rotation:	Rice-Wheat						Maize-Wheat		
Tillage:	Conventional			Reduced			Conventional		
Nitrogen Source:	In-organic Fertilizer Only	Farm-yard Manure & Fertilizer	Green Manure & Fertilizer	In-organic Fertilizer Only	Farm-yard Manure & Fertilizer	Green Manure & Fertilizer	In-organic Fertilizer Only	Farm-yard Manure & Fertilizer	Green Manure & Fertilizer
Soil Erosion (t/ha)	3.24	1.07	0.51	1.42	0.55	0.40	4.34	1.06	3.19
Rice Yield (t/ha)									
Initial	4.74	4.68	4.75	4.74	4.12	4.76			
Final	4.77	4.79	4.80	4.78	4.67	4.80			
Change	0.03	0.11	0.05	0.04	0.55	0.04			
Wheat Yield (t/ha)									
Initial	4.26	4.50	4.28	4.24	4.71	4.28	4.94	5.17	5.05
Final	4.02	4.28	4.05	4.02	4.52	4.05	4.88	5.18	5.06
Change	-0.24	-0.22	-0.23	-0.22	-0.19	-0.23	-0.06	0.01	0.01
Maize Yield (t/ha)									
Initial							3.79	3.96	3.82
Final							3.88	4.00	3.88
Change							0.09	0.04	0.06
Off-Site Costs (Rs/ha)	1,579	521	248	692	268	195	2,115	517	1554

for all systems is much greater than under current price policy. Because production costs are not subsidized, the full costs of natural resource degradation are reflected in the balance sheets. This scenario would produce the least economic distortion in the Indian context in the absence of international cooperation.

The *free world trade* scenario simulates a completely undistorted economic environment—no producer or consumer subsidies of any kind. This would be possible only if the industrial countries eliminated producer price subsidies and stopped dumping surplus production on the world market and if all countries opened their markets.

Because of the large increases in world market prices that could be expected in such an economic climate, the net financial value of all the production systems would increase. Once again, however, because resource degradation would not be subsidized, the farming systems that cause the least degradation would be the most profitable.

Net Economic Value There are two significant differences between calculations of net financial value and net economic value:

- Net economic values include the costs of cleaning up sedimentation from irrigation works.

- Net economic values are calculated from shadow prices, not market prices. Thus, each farming system has only two net economic values: one for the domestic policy options and one for the free world trade scenario.

The results presented in Table II-7 once again show that, when the productivity of natural resources is taken into account, resource-conserving farming practices are the most economical. (For illustrative purposes, results for gross operating margin, soil depreciation and groundwater depreciation are shown using market prices.)

The rice-wheat farming system that improves soil productivity, reduces groundwater depletion, and causes no off-site damage, has the largest net economic value. These values are about 20 percent higher than for the typical production system in the region, which causes the largest decline in soil productivity, maximizes groundwater depletion, and causes the most off-site damage.

The results imply that it is economical to accept a lower yield today in order to maintain production tomorrow. However, even the most economical rice-wheat system results in groundwater depletion. Other systems not tested, that may dramatically increase water use efficiency or include crops such as oilseeds that are less water-demanding, may prove to have even greater economic values.

The net economic value under the *free world trade* scenario is higher due to the higher prices that would result from opening markets and eliminating surplus dumping. Under this scenario, irrigation practices that reduce or minimize groundwater depletion by using 20 percent less water than recommended have the greatest net economic values.

Conclusions

Farming practices The predominant rice-wheat farming system in Ludhiana causes much greater environmental damage, is less profitable to farmers, and holds much less economic value for society than alternative farming systems that conserve natural resources.

Of the 20 alternative production practices tested, only 2 had a lower net financial value than one of the most common farming systems in the Punjab today. None caused greater environmental damage. In terms of social gain, the typical production system also performs poorly; only one production alternative generates a lower net economic value.

In comparison, any production system that conserves either soil or water produces greater net financial value and net economic value than the typical production system. Production systems that conserve *both* soil *and* water, damage natural resources the least and give farmers the best overall profitability and society the greatest economic gain. Under current policy, the two systems with the largest net financial values both use reduced tillage and recommended levels of irrigation. One, however, uses only inorganic fertilizers, while the other uses inorganic fertilizers and farmyard manure. Besides averting soil depreciation, the farmyard manure system adds value to the soil.

An important conclusion of this study is that, for rice production systems in Ludhiana, soil depreciation and off-site damages could be avoided but that with the irrigation technology available today groundwater depletion could not. The typi-

Table II-6. Net Financial Value of Different Farming Practices (000 Rs.)

Rice-Wheat

Farming Practice		Inorganic Fertilizer			Farmyard Manure and Inorganic Fertilizer			Green Manure and Inorganic Fertilizer		
		Conventional Tillage								
Water Use as Percent of Recommended		115	100	80	115	100	80	115	100	80
Gross	CP	219	220	206	223	224	211	223	224	209
Operating	RCS	581	582	552	595	596	567	596	597	567
Margin	RIS	159	163	152	173	177	167	163	167	156
	RCIS	521	525	498	544	548	524	536	540	512
	FWT	609	613	582	635	639	610	627	631	600
Minus Soil	CP	7	7	7	1	1	1	7	7	7
Depreciation	RCS	16	16	16	3	3	3	15	15	15
	RIS	7	7	7	1	1	1	7	7	7
	RCIS	16	16	16	3	3	3	15	15	15
	FWT	18	18	18	4	4	4	17	17	17
Minus Ground	CP	14	9	4	14	9	4	14	9	4
Water	RCS	14	9	4	39	9	4	14	9	4
Depreciation	RIS	39	27	11	39	27	11	39	27	11
	RCIS	39	27	11	39	27	11	39	27	11
	FWT	39	27	11	39	27	11	39	27	11
Net	CP	198	204	195	208	214	206	202	208	198
Financial	RCS	551	557	532	578	584	560	567	573	548
Value	RIS	113	129	134	133	147	155	117	133	138
	RCIS	466	482	471	502	518	510	482	498	486
	FWT	552	568	553	592	608	595	571	587	572

cal irrigation strategy uses at least 15 percent more water than recommended and depletes the water table level by about 0.8 meter per year. At recommended use levels the water table declines by about 0.7 meter per year. Even accepting a management strategy that accepts a reduced yield in order to cut water use by 20 percent would entail a 0.5-meter annual drop in the water table. These results suggest that, without substantial improvements in irrigation management, rice production in the Punjab cannot be sustained indefinitely. It may be in India's long-term interests to encourage a regional movement of rice production out of the Punjab to other regions with

Table II-6. Continued

									Maize-Wheat		
		Reduced	Tillage						Conventional Tillage		
Inorganic Fertilizer			Farmyard Manure and Inorganic Fertilizer			Green Manure and Inorganic Fertilizer			In-organic	Farm-yard Manure	Green Manure
115	100	80	115	100	80	115	100	80			
237	238	224	224	225	212	227	229	214	136	179	164
616	618	587	593	595	567	605	606	577	397	495	465
177	181	170	174	178	168	167	171	161	94	137	120
557	561	534	543	547	523	545	549	523	355	454	420
649	653	623	633	637	609	637	640	611	422	525	498
7	7	7	(8)	(8)	(8)	7	7	7	1	(2)	0
16	16	16	(13)	(13)	(13)	15	15	15	3	(5)	(1)
7	7	7	(8)	(8)	(8)	7	7	7	1	(2)	0
16	16	16	(13)	(13)	(13)	15	15	15	3	(5)	(1)
18	18	18	(15)	(15)	(15)	17	17	17	3	(5)	(1)
14	9	4	14	9	4	14	9	4	0	0	0
14	9	4	14	9	4	14	9	4	0	0	0
39	27	11	39	27	11	39	27	11	0	0	0
39	27	11	39	27	11	39	27	11	0	0	0
39	27	11	39	27	11	39	27	11	0	0	0
216	222	213	218	224	216	206	213	203	135	181	164
586	593	567	592	599	576	576	582	558	394	500	466
131	147	152	143	159	165	121	137	143	93	139	120
502	518	507	517	533	525	491	507	497	392	459	421
592	617	594	609	625	613	581	596	583	419	540	499

Note: Discount rate is 8 percent.

more suitable soils and climate and simultane-ously, to encourage greater production of less water-demanding crops in the Punjab.

Of the three types of natural resource costs an-alyzed in this study, by far the largest were for groundwater use. These user costs exhibited the widest range and the largest values, as high as a present value of Rs 39,000, when shadow prices were applied. Soil depreciation values were lower, never exceeding Rs 13,000, and off-site costs of dredging did not exceed Rs 2,000. Groundwater-user costs for the typical produc-tion practice in the Ludhiana district were about

Table II-7. Net Economic Values of Different Farming Practices (000 Rs.)

Farming Practice		Conventional Tillage								
		Inorganic Fertilizer			Farmyard Manure and Inorganic Fertilizer			Green Manure and Inorganic Fertilizer		
Water Use as Percent of Recommended		115	100	80	115	100	80	115	100	80
Gross Operating Margin	CP	219	220	206	223	224	211	223	224	209
	RCS	581	582	552	595	596	567	596	597	567
	RIS	159	163	152	173	177	167	163	167	156
	RCIS	521	525	498	544	548	524	536	540	512
	FWT	609	613	582	635	639	610	627	631	600
Minus Soil Depreciation	CP	7	7	7	1	1	1	7	7	7
	RCS	16	16	16	3	3	3	15	15	15
	RIS	7	7	7	1	1	1	7	7	7
	RCIS	16	16	16	3	3	3	15	15	15
	FWT	18	18	18	4	4	4	17	17	17
Minus Ground Water Depreciation	CP	14	9	4	14	9	4	14	9	4
	RCS	14	9	4	39	9	4	14	9	4
	RIS	39	27	11	39	27	11	39	27	11
	RCIS	39	27	11	39	27	11	39	27	11
	FWT	39	27	11	39	27	11	39	27	11
Minus Off-Site Costs	CP	2	2	2	1	1	1	0	0	0
	RCS	2	2	2	1	1	1	0	0	0
	RIS	2	2	2	1	1	1	0	0	0
	RCIS	2	2	2	1	1	1	0	0	0
	FWT	2	2	2	1	1	1	0	0	0
Net Economic Value	CP	464	480	469	501	517	509	482	498	486
	RCS	464	480	469	501	517	509	482	498	486
	RIS	464	480	469	501	517	509	482	498	486
	RCIS	464	480	469	501	517	509	482	498	486
	FWT	550	566	551	591	607	594	571	587	572

Table II-7. Continued

									Maize-Wheat		
Reduced Tillage									Conventional Tillage		
Inorganic Fertilizer			Farmyard Manure and Inorganic Fertilizer			Green Manure and Inorganic Fertilizer			In-organic	Farm-yard Manure	Green Manuree
115	100	80	115	100	80	115	100	80			
237	238	224	224	225	212	227	229	214	136	179	164
616	618	587	593	595	567	605	606	577	397	495	465
177	181	170	174	178	168	167	171	161	94	137	120
557	561	534	543	547	523	545	549	523	355	454	420
649	653	623	633	637	609	637	640	611	422	535	498
7	7	7	(8)	(8)	(8)	7	7	7	1	(2)	0
16	16	16	(13)	(13)	(13)	15	15	15	3	(5)	(1)
7	7	7	(8)	(8)	(8)	7	7	7	1	(2)	0
16	16	16	(13)	(13)	(13)	15	15	15	3	(5)	(1)
18	18	18	(15)	(15)	(15)	17	17	17	3	(5)	(1)
14	9	4	14	9	4	14	9	4	0	0	0
14	9	4	14	9	4	14	9	4	0	0	0
39	27	11	39	27	11	39	27	11	0	0	0
39	27	11	39	27	11	39	27	11	0	0	0
39	27	11	39	27	11	39	27	11	0	0	0
1	1	1	0	0	0	0	0	0	2	1	2
1	1	1	0	0	0	0	0	0	2	1	2
1	1	1	0	0	0	0	0	0	2	1	2
1	1	1	0	0	0	0	0	0	2	1	2
1	1	1	0	0	0	0	0	0	2	1	2
501	517	506	517	533	525	491	507	497	350	458	419
501	517	506	517	533	525	491	507	497	350	458	419
501	517	506	517	533	525	491	507	497	350	458	419
501	517	506	517	533	525	491	507	497	350	458	419
591	607	593	609	613	613	581	596	583	417	539	497

Note: Discount rate is 8 percent.

10 percent of the gross operating margin, and soil depreciation values about 5 percent.

Pricing policies Prices tell farmers what to produce and how efficiently to use natural resources and other inputs. India's agricultural policy is largely embodied in the official prices for commodities and production input. The current price set tells farmers that conserving soil and water resources is inefficient and depleting them is efficient.

Agricultural pricing reform is a must to achieve sustainability.

Agricultural pricing reform is a must to achieve sustainability. The new agricultural prices should tell farmers to use their production assets efficiently and to husband them for the future as well as for the present. This means giving farmers a fair price for their crops and eliminating production-input subsidies. It also means that electricity, water, and other inputs have to be priced so that farmers pay for all the resources they use. The current practice of determining electricity charges only by motor size, as is now done, excuses farmers from conserving water.

Research and monitoring The large natural resource costs associated with current agricultural production methods in Ludhiana suggest that large economic gains could be had through research into resource conservation. Inexpensive methods for cutting water use in rice production could be very profitable for farmers. More important, such new methods could ensure the long-term productivity of agricultural systems that rely on groundwater. Groundwater declines like those described here cannot continue indefinitely. At some point, the cost of irrigation will outweigh the benefits of rice production, and farmers will begin growing other crops simply because they use less water. At that point, the groundwater resource may have been irretriev-

ably depleted. Farmers in Ludhiana should grow crops better suited to their porous soil and low rainfall and leave rice production to farmers in more humid areas.

Further data collection and analysis of the kind presented here are critically needed. More extensive information on alternative systems, particularly those including pulses, would be very helpful. Perhaps more profitable, less resource-demanding alternatives could be identified.

In addition, research by ecologists, epidemiologists, and other non-agricultural and agricultural specialists is needed to gauge the health impacts of groundwater contamination, pesticide use, and other problems related to agricultural production. These impacts may be economically significant, but they could not be explored here for lack of information. Including other on- and off-site impacts would most likely shift the economics farther away from conventional practices.

Notes

1. The Punjab's primary sectors have consistently grown nearly twice as fast as the national average and its secondary and tertiary sectors one and one-half times faster.

2. A block is an administrative unit. Each of the state's 12 districts has an average of 10 blocks.

3. This information has not been published and is available only for 1984, 1988, and 1989.

4. Based on the annual change in groundwater balances and the brake horsepower requirements at these depths, capital and operating cost scenarios were constructed for the rice-wheat rotation under each of the three water-management options.

5. At the recommended water-use rate, switches to larger motors would occur at years 7, 15, 22, and 30; at the 80-percent rate, at years 10, 21, and 30. For these water-use options, acceler-

ated depreciation of pumping equipment would be significantly reduced. Under the 80-percent water-use option, a 30-hp motor and a deeper bore would not be needed within the 30-year time frame of this study.

6. The off-farm cost of soil erosion for each cropping practice under consideration was obtained by multiplying the quantity of eroded soil by the dredging and transportation costs per ton of soil eroded.

Technical Annex II

Annex Table AII-1. Shadow Prices of Major Inputs and Outputs

	Rice[a]	Wheat	Maize	Urea	DAP
F.o.b. Price (US$/ton)	197.1	140.2[b]	109.0[b]	161.6	167.2
International Shipping[c] (US$/ton)	21.0	41.0	41.0	41.0	41.0
C.i.f. Price (US$/ton)	218.1	181.2	150.0	202.6	208.2
Exchange Rate[d] (Rs/US$)	31.0	31.0	31.0	31.0	31.0
C.i.f. Price (Rs/ton)	6,761	5,617	4,650	6,281	6,454
Local Handling and Transport[e] (Rs/ton)	778	778	768	1,130	1,130
Shadow Price[f] (Rs/ton)	7,539	6,395	5,418	7,411 (16,111)	7,584 (16,487)

DAP = Di-Ammonium Phosphate.

a. The price of rice is for Thai 5 percent broken. The price of US$303.22 was reduced by 35 percent to allow for quality differences.
b. FOB price of wheat and maize is ex-U.S. Gulf port; for rice, ex-Bangkok.
c. The international prices relate to average monthly prices during the period April 1991 to March 1992.
d. Exchange rate of Rs 31 is the FEDAI average indicative rate of the US dollar as reported in the Reserve Bank of India Bulletin.
e. The local handling and transport charges include port clearance charges, transport cost, and marketing and distribution charges. Local transport costs were calculated as (transport costs from Port to Delhi *minus* transport costs from Ludhiana to Delhi). For details *see* text.
f. The shadow price estimated for the fertilizer urea and DAP were *divided by* the nutrient content of these fertilizers to work out the cost per ton of nutrients. These costs are given in the parentheses.

The shadow prices for rice, wheat, maize, and chemical fertilizers were derived by treating these commodities as importable on the margin. In the case of output prices, because the study region is a net surplus producer of these commodities, it was assumed that the commodities produced there compete with imported crops not in Ludhiana but at other consuming centers within India. Delhi, a major consumption and distribution center for both commodities, was taken as the competing center. Beginning with the import price (f.o.b.) of these foodgrains, international shipping charges and insurance were added to arrive at c.i.f. prices. The difference in transport charges between the port to Delhi and Ludhiana to Delhi were added to the c.i.f. price.

Under the free world trade scenario, increases in the world prices of rice, wheat, and maize were assumed, respectively, at 15, 20, and 23 percent (Krissoff, 1990). Crop output prices were derived by adjusting the import prices by the corresponding percentage change expected in the world prices.

The average operational cost was taken as a proxy for electricity generation and distribution for irrigation pumping. The Punjab State Electricity Board reports operating costs per kilowatt hour of electricity as Rs 1.03 (Government of India, 1990).

Based on estimates of water balance, geographical area, and specific yield, changes in the water table for three years were calculated (*Table II-2*). The annual recharge estimate encompasses recharge from rainfall; seepage from canals, tanks, and flood-prone areas; recharge from shallow water table areas; and recharge from surface water irrigation applied to crops cultivated in the area. The annual draft estimate is based on a census of shallow diesel and electric tubewells, other wells and deep tubewells, and estimated annual draft of each of these structures. Ludhiana's water table declined by 0.83, 1.22, and 0.98 meter, respectively, in 1984, 1988, and 1989.

Table AII-2 shows pumping capacity estimates using standard formulas for a typical farm during July, the peak period of use. The figures shown represent the current situation of overuse. The total water requirement for a typical three-hectare farm during the peak month is 3,120 millimeter-hectares per hectare or 31,200 cubic meters. Since electricity is seldom available for more than half the day, farmers must be able to pump the total desired volume of water in 12 hours. If the initial depth to water table is 8 meters, then the total initial head (depth to water table *plus* drawdown *plus* delivery head) is 11 meters.

Table AII-2. Pumping Capacity Estimate for Peak Water Use

1. Peak water-requiring month	July
2. Number of irrigations during the month	13
3. Depth of each irrigation (mm)	80
4. Peak irrigation requirement (I) (mm net of rainfall)	1,040
5. Typical farm size (ha)	3
6. Peak monthly water volume (W) (m³)	31,200
7. Average pumping hours per day (P)	12
8. Peak discharge (D)[a] l/sec	23
9. Initial depth to water table (m)	8
10. Head (total, m)	11
11. Water horse power[b]	3.37
12. Combined efficiency of pump and transmission (CE)	0.40
13. Brake horse power[c]	8.43
14. Motor BHP (1.2 BHP)	10

Note: Calculations were made using standard formulas (Bhatia, 1988).

a. $D = \dfrac{W(m^3/mo)*1000(liters/m^3)}{P(hrs)*60(sec/min)*60(min/hr)* \text{days in month}}$

b. $WHP = \dfrac{D\,(liter/sec) * Head\,(m)}{76}$

c. $BHP = WHP/CE$

According to Table AII-3, the water horsepower at this depth is then 3.37 hp. Using a combined efficiency of 0.40 for the pump and transmission (this is a conversion factor from water horsepower to brake horsepower and expresses transmission and energy losses), the motor power (expressed as brake horsepower, BHP) for the required discharge at the initial head is 8.43 hp.

Off-site costs were applied only in evaluating net economic value of each practice. Using soil erosion estimates from the soil model and several

Table AII-3. Horsepower Requirements for Water Table Depths

Depth to Water Table (m)	Total Head	WHP	BHP	Motor BHP
8	11	3.37	8.43	10
13	16	4.90	12.25	15
18	21	6.44	16.10	20
23	26	7.97	19.93	25
28	31	9.50	23.75	30

Note: Calculations were made using standard formulas (Bhatia, 1988).

simplifying assumptions, sedimentation damages were calculated for each tillage and fertilization practice *(Table II-5)*. The damage estimates were based upon the cost of removing the sediment assumed to accumulate in local irrigation canals and transporting it to agricultural fields.

The method used to estimate long-term soil productivity and develop a soil depreciation allowance is similar to the one developed in *Paying the Farm Bill* (Faeth et al., 1991). The U.S. Depart-ment of Agriculture's Erosion-Productivity Impact Calculator (Williams, 1989) was used to estimate current and future crop yields for each rotation under tillage and fertilization alternatives. Random weather was produced by the model based upon statistical averages for the area. Crop prices assumed for the various policy scenarios were used to estimate the present value of yield changes. These values were then applied against each cropping practice's gross operating margin.

III. Wheat Farming in Central Chile

**Miguel Altieri, Carlos Benito, Andres Gomez-Lobo,
Paul Faeth, Tonci Tomic, Jorge Valenzuela**

Farming in Chile has entered a new age of prosperity. Unfortunately, this prosperity may be temporary since soil erosion is sapping even the best farmlands' productivity. Indeed, soil erosion, and its effects on productivity, is the main natural resource impact explored in this study comparing the environmental and economic advantages of conventional and organic wheat farming in central Chile, where wheat is the single most important crop.

This case study looks simultaneously at both the commercial and peasant (*campesino*) agricultural economies. To give a realistic picture of the value of agricultural production, estimates of soil productivity losses are included in net income calculations for production alternatives in both sectors. The inescapable conclusion is that farmers could sustain large financial losses if soil erosion from conventional and traditional production practices continues.

Background

Chile has undertaken a drastic economic reform. Over the past two decades, protectionist policies have been abandoned, land policy has promoted security of land tenancy, export taxes have been eliminated, import tariffs have been reduced, and price protection has been eliminated for most commodities. Liberalization in trade and finance has increased the competitiveness of tradable crops.

Agricultural revitalization has brought with it strong economic growth. So dramatically have Chile's domestic and export markets for farm products grown that its agricultural trade deficit has turned into a large surplus.

Production In agriculture, the two most important expressions of these economic changes have been increased production and crop specialization. The production of wheat and fruit, Chile's main crops, has changed most of all. Between 1979 and 1989, wheat production doubled and fruit production increased by more than a third. Higher yields were responsible for these gains since the planting areas barely changed (FAO, 1990).

Wheat took up most of the 1,157,600 hectares planted to basic crops in 1987—cereals, legumes, and roots. *(See Table III-1.)* Today, wheat makes up nearly a third of all Chilean agricultural production (Ministerio de Agricultura, 1989) and occupies 41 percent of all cropland (Valdez et al., 1991). Together, wheat and fruit-growing take up well over half of Chile's cultivated land.

Agriculture and the environment Chilean farmers are known to be using more and more inputs—fertilizers, irrigation water, and, in fruit-growing, pesticides.[1] Although environmental impact data on agricultural production are practically nonexistent in Chile, research from other parts of the world suggests that intensive use of these inputs can lead to unintended pollution and ecological damage.

Table III-1. Agriculture in Chile, 1986–87

	Commercial Farming	Peasant Farming	Total
Number of Farming Units	145,126[a]	210,000	355,126
Total Cultivated Land (ha)	1,055,400	496,100	1,552,500
Use of Land (ha)			
Annual Crops	847,000	432,200	1,279,200
Vegetables and Flowers	34,100	37,400	71,500
Grains, Legumes and Roots	769,700	387,900	1,157,600
Forage Crops	43,200	6,900	50,100
Permanent Crops	209,400	63,900	273,300
Fruit and Table Grapes	125,100	34,300	159,400
Wine Grapes	45,000	2,900	67,900
Alfalfa	39,300	6,700	46.000

Source: Adapted from Echeñique and Rolando (1989).
a. Derived from Gomez and Echeñique, 1988, Annex Table III.1.

Fertilizer use, mostly urea on cereals, shot up 746 percent in Chile between 1980 and 1988 (Anon., 1990). In fact, wheat is being overtreated with inorganic fertilizers. A 62-percent increase in urea application on wheat improved yields by only 3 percent and total production by only 5 percent from 1985 to 1990 (Anon., 1990).

Peasant and commercial agriculture Wheat, like most other agricultural products in Chile, is grown on two types of farms, commercial and peasant, with vastly different cropping conditions. Both groups of farmers are major producers of import-substituting crops including wheat, corn and beans. Because of unequal land distribution, peasant farmers have benefited less than commercial farmers from Chile's agricultural progress.

Seventy-one percent of Chilean farms are smaller than 5 hectares and cover only 10 percent of the land in production. Farmers working small parcels produce 22 percent of Chile's wheat, 32 percent of its beans, 38 percent of its lentils, 59 percent of its potatoes, and 68 percent of its peas. This low-productivity peasant sector controls about 32 percent of the arable land. About 58 percent of the small farms are located on marginal lands where erosion and deforestation are inevitable (Echeñique and Rolando, 1989).

The 4 percent of all Chilean farms bigger than 40 hectares make up 44 percent of all land in production. These large commercial farms control most of the arable land and produce 78 percent of the wheat, 87 percent of the maize, and most of the fruit (Echeñique and Rolando, 1989).

Both commercial and peasant farmers use chemical inputs, particularly fertilizers, for their conventional or traditional practices, but they obtain different yields and generate different rates of soil erosion mainly because of their land location and soil quality. Peasant farmers yields are about one-third of commercial farmers.

This dichotomy in agricultural holdings and productivity has been accentuated by the spread of chemical-intensive farming methods. Commercial farmers consistently outproduce peasant farmers, whether the crop is wheat, irrigated maize, rainfed oats, sunflower, beans, or potatoes (Echeñique and Rolando, 1989).

Agricultural Policy in Chile Chilean producers of import-competing crops are not shielded from world market competition; nor are their production input purchases subsidized. In early 1988, the Chilean government reduced import tariffs from a uniform 20 percent to 15 percent (U.S. Embassy, Chile, 1990).

Chile's main policy for reducing temporary food shortages is assuring security of wheat, sugar beet, and oilseed production through a price-band system of variable tariffs based on domestic supply and demand. The system is supposed to smooth out the price fluctuations that make innovation and input decisions difficult (Ministerio de Agricultura, 1989).

Chile has no national agricultural extension agency. University and government research centers provide research focused on high-input agroexport or commercial agriculture. No agency or institution provides technical services to the entire agricultural community, including peasant farmers.

A few government programs offer technical assistance on resource-conserving practices of interest to peasant farmers. A governmental technology-transfer program targeted to small farmers reaches only 10 percent of the peasant sector, and nongovernmental organizations (NGOs) attempt-

ing to fill the gap left by government have created innovative programs for small farmers' special needs. However, a lack of resources has kept them from reaching more than 4 percent of these farmers (Echeñique and Rolando, 1989).

Study Focus

This study compares profitability, productivity, input use, and soil productivity in commercial and peasant wheat farming. Using a two-sector linear programming model of wheat production in Chile's Central Valley, conventional and organic production alternatives are compared for the commercial sector and traditional and organic production alternatives for the peasant sector. Area under cultivation, soil depreciation, labor use, and sectoral net income are reported for seven economic scenarios.

The study region, crop, and choice of production alternatives were based upon the availability of data for the main production systems and farm alternatives that could unambiguously be described as sustainable. For lack of data, a broader range of practices could not be studied. Because data were not available, off-site costs were not estimated. Instead, an analysis was undertaken to determine the level of off-site damages per ton of eroded soil that would cause a shift in the commercial cropping practices.

Information on the commercial and organic alternatives was derived from short-term agronomic studies at research centers in Chile. The various practices represent the main farming practices used in central Chile and the organic technologies available today at the experimental level (SNA, 1991; IICA, 1990; INE, 1987; and Solazar, 1985). Three conventional and organic alternatives for commercial, and two traditional and three organic alternatives for peasant wheat production vary levels of input use, substituting labor and draft power for herbicides. The combination of fertilizers and the amounts are also varied.

Organic alternatives are presented for both the commercial and peasant sectors. They involve three alternative cropping practices that differ in their degree of soil cover: 1. wheat sown broadcast with a red clover living mulch; 2. wheat furrow planted in contour rows; and 3. wheat furrow planted with a red clover sod. All three alternatives are fertilized with animal manure. No pesticides of any sort are applied. All three systems were fertilized with 15 metric tons of manure per hectare in the case of hillside peasant agriculture, and with 34.5 metric tons of manure per hectare in the case of commercial farmers in flat lands. Tables III-2 and III-3 summarize the inputs and outputs of the farming systems represented in the sectoral model (SNA, 1991; IICA, 1990; INE, 1987; Solazar, 1985, and Technical Annex, this chapter).

The upper portion of the tables specify the technical coefficients of production. The lower portion specifies average revenues, average variable costs, average gross operating margins and average net income, for current prices of 1989–90 (US$1 = 390 pesos).

Soil data in Chile are too limited to produce empirical or simulated estimates of yield losses over time. Yield losses were extrapolated from data on current yields, erosion rates, and yield loss from a similar soil type and climatological region in the United States.

The method used here to produce crop yield estimates assumes that soil productivity cannot increase over time. Other studies, using more sophisticated soil productivity-estimating methods and long-term field trials, have shown that soil productivity can increase over time. (*See*, for example, Faeth et al. 1991.) Soil may appreciate because of improved soil structure or water-holding capability.

Scenario Analysis

The results of eight scenarios run using the linear programming model are presented in Table III-4. Model solutions provide estimates of land allocation by farming practices, the production of wheat, the corresponding use of factors of production, soil depreciation, implicit wage rates for peasant farmers, labor demand, and total net income.

The model simulates the choices that commercial and peasant farmers may make to maximize their net income for a representative year. The model chooses the optimal distribution of land across practices, given each practice's crop sales, cost of production, soil depreciation, and constraints—such as the availability of land or labor within the peasant family.

Under the first scenario (A), farmers are assumed to have rejected organic production alternatives. The base assumptions represent: the existing distribution of resources between the commercial and peasant sectors; access to irrigation for commercial farmers; a discount rate of 33 percent and 10 percent, respectively, for peasant and commercial farmers; a wheat price of 43,700 pesos per ton of wheat; and an implicit wage rate of 1,200 pesos per day for a peasant's own labor (the going agricultural wage rate).

Since organic options are excluded in the first scenario, all available land is allocated to the most profitable conventional (practice 2, Table III-2) or traditional practice (practice 1, Table III-3). Net income for the peasant sector is 314 million pesos and 5,908 million pesos for the commercial sector. The results of this scenario are in line with the current farming situation in Chile.

The remaining scenarios assume that organic alternatives are available to farmers. The results of the first scenario that includes just this change (B) show that the availability of organic alternatives would probably not change commercial production practices, but could have a significant impact on how peasants farm. If peasant farmers switched to organic alternatives, net income could increase while soil erosion and negative soil productivity impacts could go down. Yet, for a variety of reasons, peasant farmers may not adopt organic practices even though they may appear most profitable: 1. they may not know about the practices; 2. they may consider them too risky; 3. they may not have enough labor to

Table III-2. Costs of Growing Irrigated Wheat on Commercial Farms, Chile, 1989–90

Item/Technology	Unit	Price	Conventional			Organic		
			(1)	**(2)**	**(3)**	**(4)**	**(5)**	**(6)**
Wheat Yields	mt/ha	43,700	4.59	5.13	4.50	3.35	3.54	3.62
Clover Yields	mt/ha	12,050				1.75		1.5
Labor Power	days/ha	1,200	12.10	5.80	8.60	17.6	20.7	20.8
Animal Power	days/ha	600	2.90	0.02	0.10	20.90	19.7	18.3
Mechanical Power	days/ha	10,000	1.90	1.40	2.40	0.59	0.59	0.59
Seeds	kg/ha	43.7	201	180	187	213	200	213
Plants	units/ha							
Fertilizers	kg/ha							
Salitre Sodico		43	315	240	800			
Urea		71	163	211	200			
Superphosphate		57	150	171				
Salitre Potasico		54	160	400	80			
Pesticides	kg/ha							
Herbicides		25	1	3	1			
Nematicides		25						
Insecticides		25	1	1	1			
Manure	mt/ha	1,500				34.5	34.5	34.5
Other Inputs	kg/ha	13				100		100
Interest	rate	0.14						
Family Labor	%	0.33						
Revenues (pesos/ha)			200,583	224,181	196,650	167,482	154,698	176,269
Operation Costs								
Labor			14,520	6,960	10,320	21,120	24,840	24,960
Animals			1,740	12	60	12,540	11,820	10,980
Mechanical			19,000	1,400	24,000	5,900	5,900	5,900
Seeds/Plants			8,800	7,900	8,200	10,600	8,700	10,600
Chemicals			42,400	56,700	52,900	0	0	0
Manure			0	0	0	22,500	22,500	22,500
Total Operating			86,460	85,572	95,480	101,910	103,010	104,190
Financial Costs			10,752	11,326	12,418	9,870	9,688	9,842
Total Variable Costs			97,212	96,898	107,898	11,1780	112,698	114,032
Credit Needs			76,800	80,900	88,700	70,500	69,200	70,300
Gross Operating Margin			103,371	127,283	88,752	55,702	42,000	62,237
Soil Depreciation			15,696	19,856	18,703	1,195	1,318	1,318
Net Income (pesos/ha)			87,675	107,427	70,049	54,507	40,682	60,919

a. Salitre Sodico — nitrate salts.
b. Salitre Potasico — potassium salts.

Table III-3. Costs of Growing Rainfed Wheat on Peasant Farms in Chile, 1989–90

Item/Technology	Unit	Price	Traditional			Organic		
			(1)	(2)	(3)	(4)	(5)	(6)
Wheat Yields	mt/ha	43,700	1.7	1.59	1.49	1.58	1.61
Clover Yields	mt/ha	12,050				1.45		1.5
Labor Power	days/ha	1,200	9.9	10	16.5	19.5	19.6
Animal Power	days/ha	600	8.1	8.2	10.2	10	9.8
Mechanical Power	days/ha	10,000	0.9	0.6	0.6	0.6	0.6
Seeds, bought	kg/ha	43.7	63.2	66.4	213	200	213
Seeds, own	kg/ha	21.9	98.8	91.6			
Fertilizers	kg/ha						
Salitre Sodico		43	185	165			
Urea		71	108	75			
Superphosphate		57	118	160			
Ammonium Phosphate		83	124	109			
Pesticides	kg/ha						
Herbicides		25	1	1			
Nematicides		25					
Insecticides		25					
Manure	mt/ha	1,500					
Clover Seeds	kg/ha	13			15	15	15
					100		100
Interest	rate	0.14					
Family Labor	%	95					
Revenues (pesos/ha)			74,290	69,483	82,585	69,046	88,432
Operation Costs (pesos/ha)							
Labor			11,880	12,000	19,800	24,921	23,520
Animals			4,860	4,920	6,120	6,000	5,880
Mechanical			9,000	6,000	5,800	5,800	5,800
Seeds/Plants			4,900	4,900	10,500	8,700	10,500
Chemicals			21,800	21,200	0	0	0
Manure			0	0	22,500	22,500	22,500
Total Operating Costs			40,560	37,020	44,920	43,000	44,680
Financial Costs			8,106	7,490	8,218	8,456	8,736
Total Variable Costs			60,546	56,510	72,938	76,377	76,936
Gross Operating Margin			13,744	12,973	9,647	(7,331)	11,496
Soil Depreciation (pesos/ha)			3,628	3,098	569	596	609
Net Income (pesos/ha)			10,116	9,875	9,078	(7,927)	10,887

a. Salitre Sodico — nitrate salts.
b. Salitre Potasico — potassium salts.

use the practices; or 4. they may ignore or under-estimate the importance of natural resource degradation.

If such a shift to organic practices in the peasant sector occurred, labor demand in the peasant sector would almost double. Peasant labor markets were not studied to see if the necessary labor is actually available, however, the maximum implicit wage rate that peasant farmers could pay themselves and their family members and still have the same net income[2] was determined. For scenario B, this maximum implicit wage rate is 1,278 pesos per day, about 7 percent more than the going local agricultural wage rate. The labor supply might be increased by raising the implicit wage rate for peasant farmers, but only an analysis of the peasant labor market could reveal the extent of any increase.

Scenario C represents the case of a fixed supply of peasant labor. Currently, for the traditional practices, about 307,000 person-days-a-year of labor is employed. When unemployed labor in the peasant sector is added to this amount, roughly 400,000 person-days per year of labor are available. Assuming this as a fixed supply, organic farming by peasants is restricted. Net income is maximized by splitting available labor between organic production and traditional production to use all available land. The constraint reflects the labor intensity of the organic alternatives. For this scenario, a wage rate of zero was used; net incomes appear higher because the value of labor is not deducted in the net income calculation.

Two scenarios (D and E) present parametric tests of the level of increases or decreases in fertilizer and pesticide prices needed to cause a shift in production patterns. Price decreases for these external inputs have no effect on commercial production patterns, but a decline of more than about 4 percent would shift the financial incentive in the peasant sector back to traditional production practices.

Price increases for fertilizers and pesticides only widen the margin of profitability between organic and traditional practices in the peasant sector. In the commercial sector, only a large (more than 80-percent) price increase would cause commercial farmers to shift to organic practices.

A baseline assumption of this analysis is that peasant farmers use much higher discount rates than commercial farmers. Scenario F assumes a reduction in peasant discount rates, mimicking poverty-alleviation programs that may provide subsidized credit, for example. In this scenario, peasant discount rates are reduced from 33 percent to 10 percent, the same as the commercial sector's. The lower discount rate might prevail if farmers' security were improved through education or credit programs. This would accentuate long-term yield losses. Soil depreciation allowances are greater, and net income goes down for both traditional and organic practices. This financial advantage implies organic practices 40-percent higher than the going wage rate.

An output price increase was also tested (Scenario G). Based on the assumption that the economic distortions caused by agricultural policy interventions throughout the world would end, a free trade scenario was represented by a 27 percent increase in the price of wheat (Krissoff et al., 1990). Under this assumption, conventional practices in the commercial sector and organic practices in the peasant sector continue to entail a financial advantage. In the commercial sector, net income increases by 50 percent; in the peasant sector, it almost triples. Soil depreciation allowances also increase with the new price.

The final test presented extends the analysis to consider net economic value to society (Scenario H). In conventional analysis, and in analyses of net income, off-site damages from soil erosion are ignored or assumed to be zero. In reality, siltation and sedimentation will cause some damage to surface waters and related economic activities such as irrigation, fishing, water treatment, water storage, and recreation. How much damage is unknown in the Chilean context.

While the actual off-site damages of soil erosion in Chile could not be determined, analysis

Table III-4. Results of Scenario Analysis with Ecological Model

	Area Cultivated (ha/yr '000)			
	Peasant		Commercial	
	Traditional	Organic	Conventional	Organic
A. Without knowledge of organic practices[a]	31	0	55	0
B. With knowledge of organic practices	0	31	55	0
With knowledge and:				
C. Peasant labor fixed; zero wage rate implied	21.4	9.6	55	0
D. Fertilizer and pesticide price decrease of 4 percent	31	0	55	0
E. Fertilizer and pesticide price increase of 83 percent	0	31	0	55
F. Discount rate of 10 percent for peasant farmers	0	31	55	0
G. Free trade — wheat price up 27 percent	0	31	55	0
H. Off-site costs of soil erosion applied at 1,450 pesos/mt (base = 0)	0	0	0	55

Note: See Technical Annex, this chapter, for elaboration of methodology and modeling details.
a. Base assumptions: peasant farmer time rate of preference (discount rate) = 33%; commercial farmer time rate of preference = 10%; base peasant labor opportunity cost = 1,200 pesos per day, and wheat price = 43,700 pesos/metric ton.
b. N.A. = not applicable.

Table III-4. Continued

Soil Depreciation		Maximum Implicit Wage Rate for Peasant Farmers	Total Labor Demand		Net Income	
Peasant	Commercial		Peasant	Commercial	Peasant	Commercial
Present Value (pesos/ha)		(pesos/day)	(person days, '000)		(million pesos per year)	
3,628	19,856	N.A.[b]	307	319	314	5,908
609	19,856	1,278	608	319	338	5,908
2,693	19,856	0	400	319	801	5,908
3,628	19,856	1,180	307	319	340	6,033
609	1,318	1,750	608	1,144	338	2,998
1,895	19,856	1,690	608	319	298	5,908
773	25,217	1,250	608	319	921	8,943
					Net Economic Value	
0	73	N.A.	0	1,144	0	3,152

was done to estimate how serious these damages would have to become before the preference for commercial wheat production would change. This was done by trial and error to identify the value for off-site damages of soil erosion that would make the net economic value of the best conventional and best organic practice coequal. This value was determined to be 1,450 pesos (US$3.38) per ton of eroded soil. Comparative values for the United States range from $0.72 to $8.89 per metric ton (Faeth et al., 1991 and Chapter V, this study).

Conclusions and Recommendations

Given the present price structure, costs, and benefits of organic methods, peasant farmers have incentives to adopt organic practices. Conversely, commercial farmers do not have enough financial incentives to switch to organic technologies. Organic practices have higher labor requirements and much lower yields in the commercial setting than on peasant farms. These two factors appear to be the principal constraints to their adoption and enhanced profitability. Some other mixes of reduced-input, soil-conserving practices may be profitable but were not examined here.

Both organic management systems show lower estimated cumulative soil losses after 30 years. In the traditional peasant systems, higher erosion rates could cause significant yield declines with time. Organic systems could keep yields relatively higher over the 30-year period because their use entails much lower rates of soil loss. For commercial farms, the organic systems exhibit lower but relatively stable yields. Yields in the conventional management systems also decline with time, reaching organic yield levels around year 20.

Although data on the environmental impacts of Chilean agriculture are incomplete, some evidence indicates that soil erosion and pesticide contamination should be cause for concern. The decline of long-term productivity or the failure to realize potential productivity as natural resources deteriorate could reduce the overall competitiveness of the Chilean agriculture and cause significant economic harm.

In the case of peasant farming, low yields trace back to poor land quality and ineffective farming methods. Poor land quality partially reflects high rates of soil erosion and land location. Soil erosion, in turn, depends on the type of farming systems used on steep slopes.

For peasants, the design and transfer of resource-conserving practices is one way to make crop production part of sustainable development. Whether significant numbers of peasants adopt part of sustainable practices, however, depends on whether appropriate systems are further developed through research and spread through extension programs. Poverty, risk, lack of knowledge, and other impediments to implementation should be identified and addressed through participatory research methods and extension services.

Peasant agricultural development and extension programs have been pioneered by NGOs and almost ignored by the government (Gomez and Echeñique, 1988). To make amends, the government should now expand the role of NGOs, taking advantage of their experience and know-how as it plans new rural development programs.

Which farming practices are adopted by commercial farmers also depends heavily on market requirements. In Chile, government interventions in commodity and input markets are minimal, and they do not appear to be a major explanation for crop patterns and factor ratios there. For this reason, whether commercial farmers in Chile adopt alternative production systems will depend more on the generation and demonstration of new farming practices than on changes in price policies.

Future agronomic research should focus on developing cost-effective practices that increase yields, reduce labor demand, and reduce soil depletion and other environmental impacts. Research should focus not only on agronomic comparisons between conventional and alternative production systems but also on criteria and indices that account for the environmental costs of each system.

This approach presupposes that environmental monitoring programs will be set up to collect necessary information. If they are, the profitability of management practices can be evaluated more realistically in light of the effects of environmental degradation brought on by agriculture.

Notes

1. Input intensity increased in line with the "California" model.

2. This implicit wage rate applies to both organic and traditional systems. In practice, the implicit wage rate is determined by adjusting the wage rate for peasant labor and rerunning the model. Adjustments are made until the net incomes of the most profitable organic and traditional practice are equal. The maximum implicit wage rate is a function of the difference in profitability between the two practices; the larger the difference, the larger the maximum implicit wage rate.

Technical Annex III

Discount Rates

The baseline study operates with the empirical premise that discount rates are 10 percent for commercial farmers and 33 percent for peasant farmers. The higher discount rate for peasants reflects their poverty and inability to wait for investments to pay back. (Benito, 1988 and 1989).

Rates of soil erosion under the different systems (Annex Table AIII-1) were calculated over a 30-year planning horizon using values derived from studies conducted in the United States in similar cropping systems and soils (Crosson and Stout, 1983; Larson et al., 1983). Actual soil productivity assessments are not available for the study region. A loss of 1 ton of soil was assumed to be equivalent to a loss of 0.008 centimeter per hectare in soil depth, and a loss of 2.54 cms of topsoil to lead to a 5.8 percent reduction in wheat production (Follett and Stewart, 1985).

Technology was taken as constant. Soils under commercial management are relatively flat (mean of 2–3 percent slope gradient), whereas peasant farmers' soils are moderately sloped (mean of 10–20 percent slope gradient).

Table AIII-1. Soil Erosion and Yields on Commercial and Peasant Farms Under Conventional and Organic Systems

Commercial System	Conventional			Organic		
	1	2	3	4	5	6
Soil Erosion	30	35	38	3	3	3
Initial Yield	4.59	5.13	4.50	3.35	3.54	3.62
Final Yield	3.48	3.74	3.19	3.26	3.45	3.52
Peasant System	Traditional			Organic		
	1	2		3	4	5
Soil Erosion	69	60		10	10	10
Initial Yield	1.7	1.59		1.49	1.58	1.61
Final Yield	0.91	0.91		1.37	1.45	1.48

IV. Pesticides, Rice Productivity and Health Impacts in the Philippines

Agnes Rola and Prabhu Pingali

The Philippines uses less pesticide than many countries,[1] but half of what it does use is concentrated on rice production. Concern about rice pesticides in the Philippines centers on their threat to human safety, ecological balance, and productivity. Prophylactic treatment early in the season disrupts the paddy ecosystem's natural ability to cope with pest infestations, so that later it is more susceptible to pest damage. Unsafe techniques for applying these highly toxic chemicals impair human health. Both side effects cut productivity.

The rice pesticides used in the Philippines belong to the extremely hazardous World Health Organization Categories I and II (extremely and moderately hazardous). Because these chemicals (including organochlorines and organophosphates) are cheap and their use is not restricted, the most dangerous pesticides account for a growing share of total consumption in the Philippines. (See Table IV-1.)

The study site, Guimba, Nueva Ecija, is located in the Central Luzon region, the rice bowl of the Philippines. Because of its proximity to Manila, Nueva Ecija is the main supplier of rice to the metropolis. Farm gate prices of rice are higher than in the other regions of the country and input prices are lower (Rola et al., 1990).

The area under rice in the wet season is approximately 300,000 hectares; in the dry season, it totals about half of that. Mean yield per hectare in Central Luzon is higher than the national average yields. The region accounted for about 18 percent of total Philippine wet-season rice production in 1991. [Basic data from Agricultural Pesticide Industries of the Philippines database (1990), Briefing Kit for the Department of Agriculture]

Crop-Protection Technologies

To minimize crop losses, researchers and policy-makers in the 1960s and 1970s usually recommended the use of chemicals, largely because other pest-control strategies had not been tested on modern plant varieties. Today, among pest-control options farmers can choose prophylactic chemical control, natural control, varietal resistance, cultural control, or integrated pest management. For rice farmers in the Philippines, natural control is the best economic strategy, according to this study.

Prophylactic Chemical Control Prophylactic chemical control involves calendar-based pesticide application, regardless of pest density or anticipated crop loss. Prophylactic control recommendations for rice were set in the early 1970s when the modern varieties then grown were susceptible to most insect pests and diseases. Since then, despite improved varietal resistance and management practices, these recommendations have hardly changed. Prophylactic chemical control has been associated with the destruction of other beneficial (predator) species; the resurgence of the treated pest populations; outbreaks of secondary pests; residues in feed, food, and the envi-

Table IV-1. Pesticide Use on Rice, the Philippines, 1987-90

		Percent of Pesticide Use on Rice Relative to Other Crops			
	Hazard Category	1987	1988	1989	1990
Endosulfan	II	40.1	49.5	56.4	64.6
Monocrotophos	I	68.5	67.7	76.7	79.4
Cypermethrin	II	64.2	44.8	62.9	59.5
Methyl parathion	I	31.0	31.7	41.8	43.2
BPMC	II	80.9	47.8	68.7	51.7
BPMC + chlorpyrifos	II	20.9	20.9	30.5	35.7
BPMC + phenthoate	II	59.4	55.4	97.4	84.4
Diazinon	II	47.7	47.7	48.4	32.2
Carbofuran	I	55.9	72.5	66.7	17.2
Azinphos ethyl	I	38.2	35.7	41.7	46.8
Chlorpyrifos	II	0.7	7.1	7.0	5.8

Source: Basic data from Agricultural Pesticide Industries of the Philippines database (1990), Briefing kit for the Department of Agriculture.

ronment; and farmer illnesses from prolonged exposure to pesticides. These problems rule out prophylactic chemical control as a sustainable pest management strategy.[2]

Natural Control Natural control is the conservation of natural enemies by preventing their destruction or preserving their habitats. Choice of plant varieties, maintenance of alternative hosts, and proper soil management are among the tactics employed to keep enough beneficial species active to control pests. Some evidence also suggests that increasing crop diversity through intercropping or polyculture reduces damage from insect pests by providing habitat for natural enemies. To take advantage of pest-predator dynamics, natural control should be practiced at community level.

Varietal Resistance Varietal resistance to rice pests is an effective means of controlling yield losses. Most modern varieties released after the mid-1970s are resistant to brown planthopper and green leafhopper and have some resistance to stemborer. Stemborers are controlled mostly by selecting early maturing varieties. Varietal resistance is particularly important in controlling viral diseases for which there are few control options of any kind and none after planting.

The interaction of natural control and resistant plant varieties is also being investigated because these two pest-control tactics are considered compatible. When used with varietal resistance, the natural control strategy could be just as successful as judicious pesticide use, except in years when there is an unusually large pest outbreak.

Cultural Control Cultural control, by definition, includes the physical manipulation of the insect environment and excludes application of chemical pesticides and the introduction of resistant varieties or natural pest enemies. Many cultural control techniques work best when cooperation extends over a large area. Cultural controls overlap with legislative control because broad cooperation may be brought about by directives from the government and local authorities. Practices for cultural control include cultivation and rotation, timing of planting and harvesting, and variation of plant density and nutrient use.

Integrated Pest Management Based on ecological principles, integrated pest management (IPM) is the use of multidisciplinary methodologies to develop agroecosystem-management strategies that are practical, effective, economical, and protective of both public health and the environment (Smith and others, 1976).

IPM is based on the idea that, below a certain pest population density or economic threshold, the cost of control measures exceeds the value of losses from pests. At farm level, pest management decision-making is determined by at least three factors (Headley, 1972), including the nature of the pest attack and the damage it causes, the range of available protective measures and information, and farmers' objectives.

To determine the economic threshold, information is needed on the extent of a pest attack (estimated by taking field samples of the pest population); the damage function, relating the level of attack to crop loss; the control function, relating the reduction in attack to the control strategy applied; the estimated crop price; and the cost of the control strategy and its application.

In the Third World, farmers do not adopt IPM readily because it is a demanding control measure (Goodell, 1984). Because IPM is labor intensive, it would also be less attractive in high-wage areas. More research and effective extension are needed to get IPM more widely adopted. Successful IPM research demands a cooperative effort by a multidisciplinary team (Goodell et al., 1987).

Study Focus

Different pest-control strategies have different ecological and health impacts, depending on the application type, amount, and schedule. In an effort to understand the broader productivity impacts of pest control and pesticide use, this case study examined the economics of four pest-con-trol strategies for rice production in one region in the Philippines. *(See Table IV-2.)* They were:

- **complete protection**, requiring on average nine sprays, three each for the vegetative, reproductive, and ripening stages of crop growth, and sometimes two sprays during the seedbed phase;

- the **economic threshold** method, requiring treatment only when a preset threshold for economic damage has been reached. Often no spraying is required or at most one or two applications;

- **natural control**, leaving pest control to the natural predator-prey dynamics of the paddy ecosystem. Management focuses on preserving or creating hospitable environments for predators through soil management, and the selection of plant varieties and alternative host species; and

- **farmers' practice** (or current local practice), spraying most commonly two or three times a season. Some farmers spray up to five times per season; others not at all.

Farmers consider the presence of pests, the degree of pest infestation (as they perceive it), and the date of transplanting critical when they time pesticide applications. A survey by the Social Sciences Department of the International Rice Research Institute (IRRI) showed that most farmers (58 percent) spray when pest infestation is heavy. But a large minority (42 percent) spray whenever pests are present, irrespective of pest density. As many as 20 percent of farmers also use other decision rules reminiscent of calendar spray schedules or complete protection treatments, such as date of transplanting and date of fertilization (IRRI, 1988).

Organophosphates, such as methyl parathion, monocrotophos and azinphos-ethyl, are the most popular pesticides among Filipino farmers. They are comparatively cheap, widely available, and known for wide-spectrum toxicity—and extremely hazardous. Many popular chemicals in

Table IV-2. Frequency of Pesticide Application, by Treatment and Season, Guimba, Nueva Ecija, 1985–88

	Wet Season (1985–87)			Dry Season (1986–88)		
Frequency	Complete Protection	Economic Threshold	Farmers' Practice	Complete Protection	Economic Threshold	Farmers' Practice
0		27	4		21	0
1		5	3		1	5
2		0	8		18	10
3			1			3
4			0			1
5			0			1
8	12			6		
9	4			8		
10	0			6		
Total	16	32	16	20	40	20

Source: International Rice Research Institute, Entomology Division (1988).

the Philippines have been banned or severely restricted in the United States.

Methodology

The methodological framework for this analysis is based on the theory of "expected utility," which estimates farmers' perceptions of the profitability and uncertainty of production. This two-part analysis first explores expected utility in terms of production costs, yield variability, and producer attitudes toward risk. In the second part, the analysis is extended to include the farmer health costs associated with each of the four alternative production practices.

The estimated productivity relationships between crop yields and crop-protection techniques were estimated first using data from experimental trials on farmers' fields in the Nueva Ecija region of the Philippines *(See Technical Annex IV-1)*. The results show that increasing fertilizer use im-

plies increased risk, while using pesticides reduces risk. Yields under the complete protection alternative consistently have the highest yields; natural control, the lowest. The absolute differences amount to less than one ton per hectare.

Yield productivity relationships were then used to calculate expected net benefits. Of the three methods used to estimate net benefits, two apply different functional forms and one simply uses the raw data means. *(See Technical Annexes IV-1 and IV-2 for details.)* Complete protection entailed the lowest risk, but cost nearly twice as much as the economic threshold method and farmers' practice. The use of a riskier but more profitable pest-control technique suggests that farmers use pesticides not to eliminate risk but to respond to their perception of pest attack. The most economical methods are farmers' practice and natural control, depending upon whether the season is wet or dry. Both practices have higher net benefits than the recommended economic thresholds or complete protection. *(See Table IV-3.)*

Table IV-3. Estimated Net Benefits of Treatments, Excluding Health Costs, (pesos/ha) by Season: Guimba, Nueva Ecija, 1985–88.

Treatment	Model I	Model II	Model III
Wet Season			
Complete Protection	11,532	12,337	12,477
Economic Threshold	12,469	12,679	12,819
Natural Control	**13,498**	13,393	13,708
Farmers' Practice	**13,497**	**13,637**	**13,917**
Dry Season			
Complete Protection	11,846	10,936	11,931
Economic Threshold	12,797	11,607	12,377
Natural Control	**14,009**	12,539	13,169
Farmers' Practice	13,847	**12,692**	**13,252**

For six input price scenarios tested for wet season production, farmers' practice always has the highest net benefit, with natural control a percent or two lower. Higher input prices have the greatest impact on the complete protection method, since that uses the highest input level. *(See Table IV-4.)*

Farmers' practice also confers the most net benefits under three output price scenarios; natural control, again, ranks close behind. The only change in ranking occurs under a high-output price scenario: complete protection then has higher benefits than the economic threshold method. In general, net returns among treatments vary less under output price changes than under input price changes. Farmers using their current practice or natural control benefit most under a scenario of high pesticide prices coupled with a high output price.

Health Costs of Pesticide Use

Exposure to pesticides can cause heart, lung, nerve, blood, and skin problems that cut productivity when farmers lose field time coping with symptoms or seeking treatment. Farmers who are unaware of these adverse effects or who attribute the symptoms to some other cause may over-

value the benefits of pesticide use and use them beyond optimal levels.

Pesticide use in lowland ricelands has become commonplace in the Philippines, even though most rice farmers have little accurate knowledge about pests and their control. Often, farmers are confused about which chemical to use, how much, and when (Huelgas, 1989). Lack of knowledge on safe pesticide handling and storage also raises farmers' risk of unnecessary exposure, poisoning, and death. Other documented unsafe pesticide practices include returning to fields too soon after spraying (Rola et al., 1992; Pingali et al., 1990; Rola, 1989).

Pesticide poisonings on farms have been observed and recorded in national statistics. In Department of Health hospitals, 4,031 cases of acute pesticide poisoning were reported, with 603 deaths, in 1980–87 (Castañeda and Rola, 1990). Because most poisonings are self-treated, the incidence of pesticide poisonings is probably underestimated.

Central Luzon farmers have reported cases of acute pesticide poisoning with symptoms including headaches, dizziness, vomiting, and stomach pain. *(See Table IV-5.)* A related study by Rola

Table IV-4. Effects of Input and Output Price Changes[a] on Net Benefits, Excluding Health Costs, by Treatment, Wet Season[b]

Changes due to					
Pesticide Price	Monitoring Labor Cost	Complete Protection	Economic Threshold	Natural Control	Farmers' Practice
Low	Low	11,812	12,749	13,813	14,057
Low	None	11,812	13,649	13,813	14,057
Low	High	11,812	12,299	13,813	14,057
High	Low	9,236	12,582	13,813	13,957
High	None	9,236	13,482	13,813	13,957
High	High	9,236	12,132	13,813	13,957
Rice Price					
Low		11,812	12,749	13,813	14,057
Medium		18,592	18,869	19,903	20,312
High		23,112	22,949	23,963	24,482

Note: All #1 entries are benchmark figures.

a. Values in pesos: low pesticide price = 234; high pesticide price = 401; no labor cost = 0; low labor cost = 1,350; low palay price = 3,500; medium palay price = 5,000; and high palay price = 6,000.
b. Results are based on Model I.

(1989) showed that about 50 percent of rice farmers reported sickness due to pesticide use.

Evidence of Health Impairments Among Rice Farmers Due to Pesticide Exposure Marquez et al. (1992) compared the health status of farmers who were exposed to pesticides and farmers who weren't. Table IV-6 compares the health impairments per organ system of Quezon farmers (the unexposed group) and Nueva Ecija farmers (the exposed group). In the exposed group, evidence of increased eye, skin, lung, cardiovascular, and neurological diseases was found.

The data used to estimate health costs were taken from a farmer survey during the 1991 dry season by the IRRI Social Science Division. Two sets of information were available from the 42 farmer-respondents in Nueva Ecija: a detailed physical and laboratory examination of each farmer, including a documented personal history of health and such habits as drinking and smoking; and technology use, especially pest-management practices, including safe handling (Marquez et al., 1992).[3]

Eye Effects Because the farmers in the Quezon group were older, more cases of pterygium (perhaps unrelated to pesticides) were expected than in Nueva Ecija. Contrary to expectations, however, more statistically significant cases were found in Nueva Ecija (67 percent) than in Quezon (11 percent).

Pesticide-related pterygium, can come about from pesticide irritation of the conjunctivae. For at least five years, the farmers in Nueva Ecija have used phenoxy herbicides and acetamides, both known to be moderately irritating to the eye. Nueva Ecija farmers have frequently applied highly concentrated forms of both 2,4-D and acetamides.

Table IV-5. Number of Poisoning Cases, as Reported by Farmers, Nueva Ecija, 1989 Dry Season

Symptom[a]	Number	Percent[b]
Headache, dizziness	35	69
Vomiting	12	24
Unconsciousness	8	16
Stomach Pain	5	10
Weakness	3	6
Others	3	6
Total Victims[c]	51	
Total Respondents	60	

Source: Unpublished data, Social Sciences Division, IRRI.

a. Multiple responses.
b. Cases reported/total victims.
c. As reported by respondents.

Skin Effects Almost half (46 percent) the Nueva Ecija farmers showed dermal impairments, compared to none of the farmers from Quezon. One third (37 percent) of Nueva Ecija farmers, but none from Quezon, exhibited nail destruction—perhaps due to the use of organotins as molluscicides used against snails. Organotins were banned in the Philippines and replaced by endosulfan, a substitute molluscicide. Later, endosulfan was prohibited for use on golden snails, for which it is not registered.

Respiratory Tract Effects No significant number of farmers (7 percent) in Nueva Ecija had bronchial asthma, and none in Quezon did. Other abnormal respiratory findings were significantly more prevalent in Nueva Ecija (40 percent) than in Quezon (23 percent).

Cardiovascular Effects There was no significant difference in electrocardiograms (EKGs) of farmers at the two sites. Stratifying results to account for differences in age and drinking gives a totally different picture. Both factors, known to adversely affect cardiovascular outcomes, were unequally distributed in the study groups, and they can confound the result. When age was held constant, nobody under 40 years of age in Quezon had abnormal EKGs, but 39 percent in Nueva Ecija did. Normally, EKG changes would be more prevalent among people over 40. Holding drinking constant, 11 percent in Nueva Ecija had functional EKG impairments but none in Quezon. Further stratifying the sample by sex, all but two cases of cardiac abnormalities were males. Because young males customarily apply the pesticides, they are at an abnormally higher risk for cardiac disorders than older males. No significant difference in blood pressure elevation between the two groups was reported.

Neurological Effects No one in Quezon had polyneuropathy; 11 percent in Nueva Ecija did. There was a significant difference between the results in Quezon and in Nueva Ecija. Nueva Ecija farmers were heavy users of both monocrotophos and 2,4-D, which explained the higher prevalence of the disease in Nueva Ecija. Taking drinking into account, 8 percent of farmers from Nueva Ecija had polyneuropathy; none from Quezon did.

Forty percent of the control group had one pesticide-related impairment; 32 percent of Nueva Ecija farmers had four. The maximum number of health problems in the Quezon group was four; in the Nueva Ecija group, seven. Farmers and agricultural workers thus face chronic health effects from prolonged exposure to pesticides. Eye, skin, nail, pulmonary, neurological, and renal problems are significantly associated with long-term pesticide exposure in this area.

Estimating Health Costs To estimate how pesticide exposure could affect net benefits, a health-cost function was estimated using medical and social data on rice farmers from the same experimental area *(See Technical Annex IV-2).* The health-cost estimates were developed using detailed physical and laboratory examinations of the Nueva Ecija farmers and information on their pesticide-use practices, pesticide exposure, and

Table IV-6. Health Impairments Among Quezon and Nueva Ecija Farmers

Organ/System Health Indicators	Quezon Control Group (39 individuals)		Nueva Ecija Exposed Group (57 individuals)	
	Number	Percent	Number	Percent
Eyes (pterygium)	4	10	38	67
Skin (nail pitting, eczema)	0	0	26	46
Respiratory	9	23	26	46
Cardiovascular (elevated BGP, EKG)	18	46	28	49
Gastrointestinal Tract (GIT) (chronic gastritis)	0	0	5	9
Kidneys (albuminuria, hematuria elevation of creatinine)	10	26	20	35
Neurologic System (polyneuropathy, isolated hypo/hyper/areflexia)	10	25	20	35
Hematologic System (low hemoglobin, thrombocytopenia, lymphocytosis)	29	74	51	89
Cholinesterase Baseline	0	0	0	0

Note: Percentages for kidneys, the neurologic system and cholinesterase baseline, are not statistically significant between the two groups.

Source: C.B. Marquez, P.L. Pingali, and F.G. Palis, 1992.

the hazard category of the pesticides used. Treatment costs were computed based on the medical test results and the costs of restoring the individual to normal health (medication, physicians' fees, plus the opportunity cost of the farmer's time during recovery).

The results of this analysis reveal that the level of insecticide dose significantly affects health costs, while the level of herbicide dose does not. One explanation is that farmers mostly use pesticides in the most dangerous I and II categories but use herbicides in the less dangerous categories III and IV. Health costs increase 0.74 percent for every 1 percent increase in pesticide use.

Expected health costs for each treatment were estimated using the health-cost function developed. Since the natural control method uses no pesticides, the associated health costs are zero. Under farmer practice, health costs increase by 623 pesos in the wet season and, in the dry, to 1,188, almost 10 percent of net benefits. The highest dosage levels are for the complete protection method, as is the highest incremental health cost. In the wet season, health costs would increase by 6,735 pesos; in the dry season, by 7,450 pesos—almost 60 percent of prior net benefits.

These health costs, when added to other production costs, cause a shift in the net benefits so that natural control has higher net benefits than the other treatments, including farmer practice. Complete protection has 50-percent lower net benefits than the others. The results also imply that farmers who considered health costs would increase threshold levels for spraying. *(See Figure IV-1 and Table IV-7.)*

Conclusions and Recommendations

Several key conclusions can be drawn from the results.

Under normal circumstances, the natural pest control option is often the most economi-

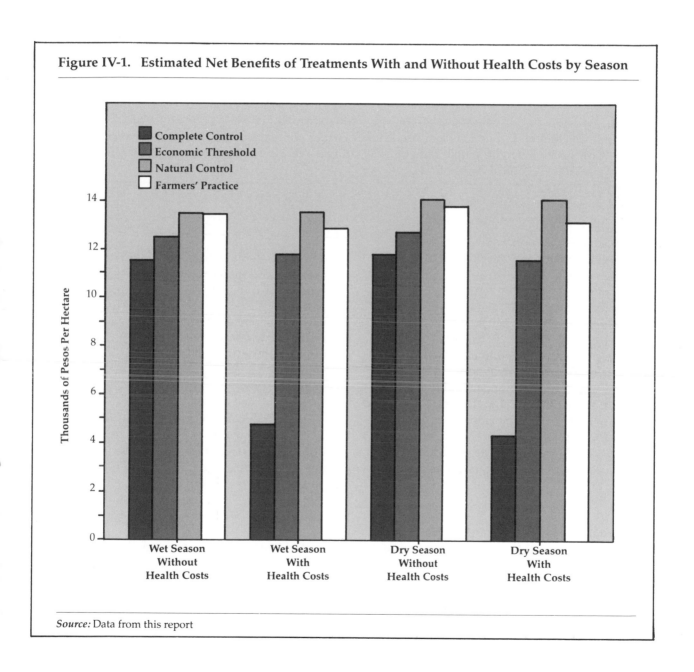

Figure IV-1. Estimated Net Benefits of Treatments With and Without Health Costs by Season

Source: Data from this report

Table IV-7. Net Benefits[a] of Pesticide Treatment, Including Health Costs, Nueva Ecija Rice Farmers

Treatment	Model I	Model II	Model III
Wet Season			
Complete Protection	4,797	5,602	5,742
Economic Threshold	11,822	12,032	12,172
Natural Control	**13,498**	**13,393**	**13,708**
Farmers' Practice	12,874	13,014	13,294
Dry Season			
Complete Protection	4,396	3,486	4,481
Economic Threshold	11,609	10,419	11,189
Natural Control	**14,009**	**12,539**	**13,169**
Farmers' Practice	13,127	11,972	12,532

a. Based on estimates of nonsmoker/nondrinker farmer population and assuming an average age of 48.69 years, a weight/height ratio of 24.79, and an average herbicide dose of 1.79. Models are as defined in Technical Annex IV-1.

cal. Natural control conserves natural pest enemies, preventing their destruction and preserving their habitat. Working with the agroecosystem, instead of against it, generates the greatest benefits.

When pesticide-related health costs are accounted for, natural control dominates even for risk-averse farmers. Prolonged and frequent exposure to pesticides damages farmers' health and productivity. Health impairments are directly related to the application frequency. Thus, the more pesticides used, the higher the pesticide-related health costs. The value of crops lost to pests is invariably lower than the cost of pesticide-caused health problems.

Alternative pest-management strategies should be developed based on a broad ecological and long-term approach. Crop rotation, timing of pesticide application, and other factors that will minimize outbreaks and losses from insect pests should be considered. Health impacts should be explicitly studied as part of pest-management research.

Pest-related yield losses depend on agroclimatic conditions, cropping intensity, varieties used, land and crop management practices, and pest control methods. Since crop-loss assessments vary widely by location and year, single-period assessments done at one spot cannot be generalized over time and place. Long-term loss assessments have generally shown modest yield losses to insect pests.

National pesticide policies should restrict use of the most hazardous pesticides in rice production. More discretion should be used in importing and licensing agrochemicals. Chemicals that persist in the paddy environment, harm aquatic life, and induce pest resurgences should be banned in favor of safer chemicals.

Removing all explicit and implicit subsidies on pesticides is essential to reduce pesticide use on farms. Taxes on pesticides can be used to reduce farmers' health risks. For instance, if governments tax the highly toxic Category I and II chemicals heavily enough, farmers may switch to the less hazardous Category III and IV chemicals.

Notes

1. Pesticide use for rice production in Asia varies dramatically by country. At one end of the continuum is Japan, with an average of more than 14 kilograms of active ingredient per hectare; at the other is India, with just 0.33 kilograms per hectare. Globally, more pesticides are used on rice than on any other crop. Rice pesticides account for US$2.4 billion in sales, nearly 15 percent of the pesticide market worldwide.

2. Due to unilateral chemical use and crop intensification, epidemics of brown planthopper and green leafhopper and their associated viral diseases spread throughout the rice-growing Philippines (Litsinger, 1987). Brown Planthopper (BPH) [*Nilaparvata lugens*] is the preeminent insect pest of the modern Green Revolution (Kenmore and others 1984). Planthoppers, by eating rice plants, cause a symptom known as "hopperburn" (Heong, 1991). These pests were major threats to rice cultivation in the 1960s and 1970s. They are still considered the single most important insect problem plaguing rice production today (Teng, 1990). Among the factors contributing to the increase and severity of BPH outbreaks, pesticide-induced resurgence is of major importance. Many commonly-used pesticides for rice insect control in Asia caused the BPH resurgence. For instance, Reissig and others (1982) found that 16 of the 39 pesticides tested caused BPH resurgence.

   Kenmore and others (1984) also showed that disrupting population-regulating factors such as natural enemies, especially by pesticides, can induce tropical BPH population outbreaks. Neither varieties *per se* nor fertilizer levels have been shown to induce BPH outbreaks, but destroying natural enemies with pesticides does so consistently if enough BPH are active in the vicinity. Kenmore (1980) reported that nearly every recorded outbreak of BPH in the tropics has been associated with prior use of pesticides.

3. The medical assessment was done by a team consisting of a physician, a nurse, an X-ray technician, and medical technologists. The nurse interviewed the farmers about their personal, family, and occupational histories, as well as their drinking and smoking habits. The doctor did a complete physical examination on every farmer. Cholinesterase determination was done by the medical technologist, chest X-rays and electrocardiograms were done by the X-ray technician.

Technical Annex IV-1

Methodology

The concepts of production risk, defined in terms of randomness in production, and farmer attitude toward risk, defined in terms of the utility function, can be used to generalize the neoclassical efficiency and welfare analysis. The distribution of output, conditional on management decisions, replaces the neoclassical production function. The maximization of expected utility of profit replaces the profit-maximization postulate of the neoclassical model. Expected utility then is maximized by choosing the level of input at which an additional or marginal unit of input gives no higher utility.

Theoretical Framework

It is assumed that in production decisions, farmers behave as if they maximize the mathematical expectation of utility and that utility is a function of profits, among other variables. Expected utility is based on the decisionmaker's subjective probability distributions of the random variable in profit. It is further assumed that profit variability is directly related to output variability which is directly related to insect-damage variability among other variables.

Hence, the objective is to maximize

(1) $E u(\pi) = E u (py - wx) = u (x,a,w,s)$, where:

> u = (π ,s), the decisionmaker's utility function;
>
> π = profit or net benefit and s is the parameter vector defining the utility function;
>
> p = output price, assumed to be predetermined and constant across experimental treatments;
>
> y = yields, a random variable, whose distribution is conditionally defined on the input vector x;

> w = a vector of input prices, usually predetermined;
>
> x = input vector to be chosen;
>
> a = a vector of parameters which with x define the probability distribution of y.

The solution to the expected utility maximization problem is $x^* = x^* (a,s,w)$.

Estimation Procedure

Yield Distribution Function. Two models were used to derive for probability distribution of yields, y.

Model I: Just and Pope (1979)

The Just and Pope model specifies the following relationship:

(2) $y = f(x) + h(x)^{1/2}e^u$, where

> y = yield,
>
> $f(x)$ = deterministic component of the production function;
>
> x_1 = is log fertilizer (in kilograms) x_2 is insecticide (in dosage level), x_3 is season dummy, where
>
> $h(x)$ = stochastic component of the production function, and
>
> e^u = error term,

where both f and h follow a popular log-linear form—the Cobb-Douglas. The function f(x) could be estimated using the nonlinear regression estimation and h(x) is estimated using the ordinary least squares.

The second moment or variance of the distribution was computed via a weighted regression of the inputs of production by the square of the error term in (2). Means and variance of yields

Annex Table AIV-1-1. Estimated yield distribution function for experimental plots, Guimba, Nueva Ecija, 1985–1988 in logarithms and using Just and Pope model

Parameter	Moments	
	1st	2nd
Constant	1.02***	-0.01
	(6.32)	(-0.29)
Log Nitrogen	0.09***	0.009
	(2.38)	(1.24)
Pesticide Dosage	0.007***	-0.002*
	(2.72)	(-1.85)
Season Dummy	-0.087*	0.042***
	(-1.76)	(2.46)
F-value	4.39***	31.15***
	(3.132)	(4.119)

Note: Figures in parentheses are t-values.
***Significant at 1 percent level.
** Significant at 5 percent level.
*Significant at 10 percent level.

and net benefits were estimated using the Just and Pope model fitted to the raw data.

Model II: Log-linear equation with treatments as intercept shiftors

The second model used to estimate yield distribution is a log-linear model where each technology is represented by a treatment dummy. Hence:

$$(3)\ lny\ =\ f(lnN, SD, TD_1, TD_2, TD_3, TD_4),\ where:$$

y = yield of rice per hectare;

lnN = log of nitrogen;

SD = season dummy, where SD

= 0 for wet season and

= 1 for dry season

TD_1 = dummy for complete protection;

TD_2 = dummy for economic threshold;

TD_3 = dummy for natural control;

TD_4 = dummy for farmers' practice.

Net Benefit or Profit Function

Once the yield distribution function is estimated, a net benefit function could be defined by the following standard form:

$$(4)\ \pi\ =\ py - wX,\ where:$$

p = price of the output;

Y = stochastic yield;

w = vector of input prices; and

x = vector of input use.

Table AIV-1-2. Estimated yield distribution functions for Guimba, Nueva Ecija, 1985–1988, in logarithms, with treatments as intercept shiftors.

Parameter	Moments	
	1st	2nd
Log Nitro	0.09***	0.006
	(2.73)	(0.62)
Season Dummy	-0.08	0.028**
	(-1.84)	(2.30)
Dummies for:		
Complete Protection	1.16***	-0.016
	(7.99)	(-0.39)
Economic Threshold	1.02***	0.014
	(7.17)	(0.34)
Natural Control	0.99***	0.010
	(6.86)	(0.23)
Farmers' Practice	1.02***	-0.003
	(7.09)	(-0.08)
R^2	0.98	0.40

Note: Figures in parentheses are t-values.
***Significant at 1 percent level.
** Significant at 5 percent level.
*Significant at 10 percent level.

Moments of net benefits are directly related to moments of yields because p, w, and X are assumed to be predetermined variables, and y is the only stochastic component of the equation. In addition, the yield distribution function reflects the stochastic effects of insect damage on production and hence indirectly on yields.

Expected Utility Function To implement welfare and efficiency analysis, a utility function must be specified over a range of farmer population. If utility depends only on a single attribute, the utility function can be respecified as an expected utility function defined in terms of the moments of the probability distribution of that single attribute.

Following Anderson, Dillon, and Hardaker (1980), the basis-of-the-moment method is a Taylor series expansion, with the equation of the expected utility function expressed as follows:

$$(5)\ E[U(\pi)] = U[E(\pi)] + U_2[E(\pi)]M_2(\pi)/2 + U_3[E(\pi)]M_3(\pi)/6 + \ldots \text{where:}$$

U = functional form of the utility function;

U_2, U_3 = the second and third derivatives of the utility functions;

M_2, M_3 = the second and third moments of the probability distribution functions of the attribute, say profit (π).

Empirically, it could be shown that terms beyond the first three moments of the distribution add insignificantly to the precision of the approximation.

To translate these estimates to expected utility framework, Sillers (1980) values of partial risk aversion parameters were used. He obtained these values experimentally from rice farmers in Nueva Ecija, the same province as the farmers in this study. The elicitation method consisted of a series of experimental games, in which subjects were confronted with choices among sets of alternative prospects or gambles, involving real money pay-offs. The rounds, at first, involved small amounts of money, and the pay-off scale increased in later rounds. In the final round, the subjects faced potential pay-offs comparable to returns on major agricultural investments and annual incomes for most farm households in the area at that time.

Parallel experimental games were conducted in two villages with similar socioeconomic characteristics. One set involved only gains to the subjects; the other involved both gains and losses. The games were designed with different odds for winning or losing to test the importance of probability preferences. Sillers's results showed that the higher the pay-offs, the more risk averse the farmer becomes.

To compute for expected utility of net benefits, it is assumed that the farmer operator's utility function is negative exponential. Following Sillers (1980), this can be expressed as:

$$U(\pi) = (1\text{-}S)\,\pi^{(1-S)},$$

where $U(\pi)$ = utility of net benefits

S = risk aversion parameter.

The expected utility function can then be expressed as:

$$(EU(\pi) = (1-S)\pi^{(1-S)} + (1-S)^2\pi^{-S}\frac{V(\pi)}{2} - S(1-S)^2\pi^{-(1+S)}\frac{M3(\pi)}{6},$$

where:

$EU(\pi)$ = expected utility of net benefits;

$V(\pi)$ = variance of net benefits, and

$M3(\pi)$ = third moment of net benefits.

The third fragment of the equation (that is, containing M3) was not included in the computations, because the values derived from it were negligible.

Technical Annex IV-2

Reestimating Expected Utility Function Incorporating Health Costs Due to Pesticide Exposure

Theoretical Framework

Incorporating health costs into the expected utility function would entail a shift of this function to the left. Hence, the objective function in Chapter IV can be rewritten as:

$$E U(\pi) = E U(py - wx - HC) = u(x, a, w, s),$$
where:

U = $U(\pi,s)$, the decision maker's utility function;

π = is profit or net benefit and s is the parameter vector defining the utility function;

p = output price, assumed to be predetermined and constant across experimental treatments;

y = output, a random variable, whose distribution is conditionally defined on the input vector x;

x = input vector to be chosen;

w = a vector of input prices, usually predetermined;

a = a vector of parameters which with x define the probability of y; and

HC = health cost as a result of illness due to pesticide exposure.

HC estimation is described below. The values of HC are used to recompute for the values of net benefits and certainty equivalents by treatment and by season.

The Health Cost Model and Estimation Procedure

Health costs from pesticide use would be associated with: total pesticide use; pesticide exposure (the number of times the farmer comes into contact with pesticides); pesticide hazard category, (Category I and II pesticides, such as those listed in Table IV-1) most organophosphates and organochlorines have a greater effect on health than Category III or IV pesticides; and "other" farmer characteristics (weight over height, age, smoking, and alcohol consumption and a proxy for nutritional status).

The log-linear equation in the following form was used in the estimate:

ln HC	= f (LAGE, WTHT, DS, DD, LOG TOT DOSE, L DOSE I, LDOSEH) where:
ln HC	= log of health costs, in pesos;
LAGE	= log of farmers' age;
WTHT	= farmers' weight by height;
DS	= dummy for smoking, where DS = 0 for nonsmokers and 1 for smokers;
DD	= dummy for drinking alcohol, where DD = 0 for nondrinkers and 1 for drinkers;
LOG TOT DOSE	= log of total dosage of pesticides used including insecticides, herbicides and other pesticides in active ingredient per hectare (a.i./ha);
LDOSEI	= log of insecticides used, in a.i./ha
LDOSEH	= log of herbicide used, in a.i./ha.

Pesticide category was not included in the equation since most pesticides used are in Category I or II; most herbicides, in Category III and IV. Pesticide exposure is also reflected in the pesticide dose variables. Total dosage, pesticide dosage, and herbicide dosage were standardized by using the strength of formulation (recommended active ingredient) as the weights.

Annex Table AIV-2-1. Estimated Health Cost Distribution, Rice Farmers, Nueva Ecija, Dry Season, 1991

Independent Variables	Equation (1)	Equation (2)	Equation (3)
Intercept	-0.23 (-0.06)	-2.28 (0.63)	1.33 (.36)
Log of Age	1.97[b] (2.22)	2.35[a] (2.67)	1.82[b] (2.17)
Weight by Height	-0.03 (-0.57)	-0.02 (-0.50)	-0.05 (-1.06)
Dummy for Smoking	1.15[a]	0.97[b]	1.10[a]
Drinking	-0.80[c]		-0.77[c]
Log of Total Dose			0.62[b] (2.31)
Log Dose Pesticide	0.74[c] (1.75)	0.72[c] (1.65)	
Log Dose Herbicide	0.46 (0.47)	0.53 (0.52)	
R^2	.40	0.35	.43

Note: Dependent variable is log of health cost. Figures in parentheses are not values.
a. Significant at = .01.
b. Significant at = .05.
c. Significant at = .10.

V. Alternatives to Corn and Soybean Production in Two Regions of the United States

Paul Faeth and John Westra

U.S. agricultural policy was designed to make sure that consumers have enough reasonably priced food and fiber and that producers earn an adequate income (Becker, 1988). However, plans have gone awry. Oversupply has become a chronic problem, and consumers pay huge fiscal, economic, and environmental costs to support farm income. Moreover, the way policy is administered virtually forces farmers to deplete the natural resources on which future supplies depend (Phipps and Reichelderfer, 1988).

Direct government payments to producers in fiscal year 1993 will be more than $17 billion (USDA, 1993), and higher food prices cost U.S. consumers $10 billion (Bovard, 1989). These figures do not include the costs of damage to natural resources by agricultural runoff, estimated at close to $4 billion a year just for surfacewater (Ribaudo, 1989).

The complex web of restrictions and compliance requirements of agricultural programs in the United States gives farmers strong incentives to use production practices that increase soil erosion and agrochemical use (Phipps and Reichelderfer, 1988). Government income support payments to farmers are calculated mainly in proportion to their land area in production, the crop grown, and the yield. Therefore, farmers with large farms and high yields from a small set of "program crops"[1] receive more support monies than farmers with small farms and low yields or nonprogram crops. Farmers who manage soil fertility and pests without using chemicals by growing nonprogram crops such as clover or alfalfa receive no government support for those crops: basically, they are penalized.

U.S. agriculture has been transformed from diversified, crop-livestock operations to specialized production systems, heavily dependent on external inputs. Over the last 30 years, pesticide use in the United States has tripled, and synthetic fertilizer use has nearly doubled, while the land area devoted to farming has barely changed at all (Phipps and Reichelderfer, 1988). Producers' increased reliance on agrochemicals has hidden the loss in soil productivity due to soil erosion and off-site damages to surface and groundwaters (Poincelot, 1986).

The impacts of agricultural policy on resource-conserving cropping practices were examined for two states, Pennsylvania and Nebraska, in an earlier World Resources Institute report, *Paying the Farm Bill* (Faeth et al., 1991). Both case studies showed that policy works against agricultural sustainability. When the soil-related resource costs of agricultural production are added to the usual business-accounting costs, U.S. farm income support programs discourage resource-conserving practices. Base acreage constraints and commodity programs that cover only seven crops put resource-conserving crop rotations at a financial disadvantage, despite the big economic gain to society from farming practices that reduce soil erosion and improve soil productivity. Moreover, the conventional, subsidized practices can cause society large net economic losses through soil erosion or damage to recreation, fisheries, and navigation.

The original study showed that if policy distortions were corrected through multilateral free trade policy, for example, net farm income and net economic value could increase considerably for both conventional and alternative practices. In Pennsylvania and other high resource-cost areas, resource-conserving practices would become most profitable options—greatly encouraging their adoption. In low resource-cost areas, such as Nebraska, even though farmers would not necessarily change practices, they would benefit from the higher crop prices expected to prevail under worldwide free trade. As a result, the population at large would suffer fewer adverse environmental impacts from agriculture, government expenditures for income support could be dramatically cut, and farm income could be maintained or improved.

Analytical Update The study reported here extends the earlier case studies for Pennsylvania and Nebraska. The policy analysis is updated to include changes in the latest revision of basic agricultural legislation, the Food, Agriculture, Trade, and Conservation Act of 1990 (FACTA), and a major proposal for the General Agreement on Tariffs and Trade (GATT). The methodology is also extended to cover the value of potential damages caused by global warming from the release of soil carbon to the atmosphere. (*See* Technical Annex for details on the methodology.)

Measuring Sustainability

The economic and resource accounting models used in this study integrate information at four levels, corresponding to the fourfold hierarchy of sustainability defined by Lowrance et al. (1988): field, farm, region, and nation. They represent in a consistent framework the farmer's financial perspective and wider environmental and economic perspectives.

At *field level*, the EPIC model developed by the U.S. Department of Agriculture (USDA) was used

to simulate the physical changes in the soil under different agronomic practices. EPIC, a comprehensive model developed to analyze the erosion-productivity problem, simulates erosion, plant growth, nutrient cycling, and related processes by modeling the underlying physical processes.

A simple farm-level programming model was developed to assess the impact of commodity programs—operating through changes in input and output prices, acreage constraints, and deficiency payments—on net farm income and net economic value. Output from EPIC was used in the programming models, which calculate not only crop sales, production expenses, government deficiency payments, and net farm incomes for each cropping pattern, but also soil-erosion rates, off-site damages, and a soil-depreciation allowance.

At *farm level*, EPIC estimates of soil productivity changes were used to calculate the economic depreciation of the soil resource. These estimates were combined with agronomic production data to determine more complete on-farm production costs for each rotation and treatment. The farm-level information on soil erosion was coupled with *regional* estimates of off-site damage per ton of eroded soil (Ribaudo, 1989) to derive estimates of off-farm soil erosion damages resulting from each agronomic practice.

At the *national level*, crop prices from agricultural sector models developed by the Food and Agricultural Policy Research Institute were used to represent the economic impacts of the various policies (FAPRI, 1988; 1990; 1992). These prices were used in farm-programming models to determine net farm income and net economic value. The farm-level model also generated estimates of government payments for the different crop production alternatives under the policy scenarios, which were generalized to compare the relative federal budgetary costs of different policy options.

Estimating a soil-depreciation allowance Estimates of the long-term soil-productivity changes from different farming practices were used to compute the present value of economic impacts of soil-productivity changes due to soil erosion and changes in soil structure. *(See Technical Annex.)* The prices used to calculate the value of the productivity changes were those projected by FAPRI for each policy scenario.

Off-farm costs of soil erosion Ribaudo (1989) has presented a comprehensive estimate of the widely varying off-site costs of soil erosion for different areas in the United States. In the Northeast, where many rivers drain into the densely populated seaboard and the economic value of water is high, the damage per ton of erosion is $8.89 (1992 dollars). At the other extreme, in the sparsely populated, dry Northern Plains, where the economic value of water is low, damage per ton of erosion is $0.72. These estimates were combined in this study with EPIC erosion estimates to calculate off-farm damages from soil erosion for the various rotations. The erosion

rates were weighted by the crop set-aside requirements for the various policy scenarios and multiplied by the regional per-ton damage estimates. These values are shown as the off-farm costs in Tables V-1 and V-2, column 2.

In Pennsylvania, for the first five years of data, crop yields in the alternative rotations were lower than conventional rotations. Possible reasons for this include: rotation adjustment, biological transition, or inexperience. In the second five years, crop yields in alternative rotations were equal to or surpassed those of conventional rotations. The first five-year period is referred to as the "transition" period, the second five-year period is called the "normal" period. The economic analysis was separated into two five-year periods, with the fifth year overlapping in order to accommodate this difference.

Cost of economic damages from soil carbon loss Numerous studies have implicated agriculture as

---

Box V-1. Rotations Compared, Pennsylvania and Nebraska

Pennsylvania—Five-Year Rotations

CC	Continuous conventional corn, herbicide and inorganic fertilizer use
CCBCB	Conventional corn-soybean rotation, herbicide and inorganic fertilizer use
ACG	Alternative cash grain, corn-corn-soybean wheat/clover-barley, organic production with mechanical weed control and green manure plowdown
ACGF	Alternative cash grain with fodder production corn-soybean-wheat/clover-clover-corn silage, organic production with mechanical weed control and animal manure plowdown
ALLHAY	Continuous alfalfa production with no fertilizer or pesticides

Nebraska—Four-Year Rotations

CC	Conventional continuous corn with herbicide and inorganic fertilizer use
HFCB	Conventional corn-soybean rotation with herbicide and inorganic fertilizer use
FOCB	Corn-soybean rotation with inorganic fertilizer use only, no herbicides
ORGCB	Corn-soybean rotation with no herbicide or inorganic fertilizer use, animal manure applied during the corn year
HFROT	Corn-soybean-corn-oats/clover, herbicides and inorganic fertilizer use
FOROT	Corn-soybean-corn-oats/clover, inorganic fertilizer use but no herbicides
ORGROT	Corn-soybean-corn-oats/clover, organic rotation with manure application

Table V-1. Rotation Characteristics, Pennsylvania

Tillage/Rotation	Soil Erosion (t/ac/yr)	Off-Farm Erosion Cost[a] ($/ac/yr)	Soil Depreciation ($/ac/yr)	Loss of Soil Carbon (t/ac/yr)	Carbon Loss Cost[b] ($/ac/yr)
Conv. Tillage					
Continuous Corn	9.26	74	25.9	0.15	5.9
Corn Beans	6.07	50	24.4	0.15	5.9
ACG	4.25	34	(2.5)[c]	0.09	3.6
ACG with Fodder	3.29	27	(7.9)	0.06	2.5
All Hay	0.66	6	(3.8)	—	
Reduced Tillage					
Continuous Corn	7.15	57	25.5	0.12	4.8
Corn-Beans	5.29	43	23.7	0.12	5.0
ACG	3.49	28	(3.4)[c]	0.08	3.1
ACG with Fodder	2.49	20	(9.5)[c]	0.05	1.9

ACG = Alternative cash grain: organic corn-corn-beans-wheat/clover-barley; ACG with fodder = organic corn-beans-wheat/clover-clover-corn silage.
a. Estimated using a damage cost of $8.89 per ton. Off-farm costs are weighted by crops and set-aside acreages that apply under FACTA. *See Table V-3.*
b. Cost estimated at $40 per ton of carbon lost.
c. Parentheses indicate appreciation in soil asset values due to increased productivity.

a key source and potential sink for greenhouse gases (Tans et al., 1990; Goudrian, 1991). The principal sources of emissions from agriculture are carbon dioxide from deforestation and soil carbon mineralization, methane emissions from rice paddies and livestock, and nitrous-oxide emissions from nitrogenous fertilizers.

To assign a value to the potential economic impact due to global warming from the various production systems, estimates of soil carbon loss from the EPIC model were combined with a carbon emission value. Dower and Zimmerman (1992) surveyed a number of studies estimating the macroeconomic consequences of controlling carbon dioxide emissions, a major greenhouse gas. These studies estimated the carbon tax rate required to reduce carbon dioxide emissions to specified levels. These tax estimates ranged from $40 to $500 per ton of carbon.[2]

A low-end estimate was used in conjunction with estimates of soil carbon losses from EPIC *(Tables V-1 and V-2, column 4)* to develop costs of soil carbon loss from the various production alternatives *(Tables V-1 and V-2, column 5)*. Estimates of soil carbon loss from EPIC compared well with empirical measurements from the field sites in Pennsylvania and Nebraska.

The carbon cost estimates were not used in the accounting framework because the carbon tax rates are uncertain, but the carbon loss estimates suggest that, for continuously cultivated land, the soil carbon losses and warming impacts are small relative to other sources. Additionally, the poten-

Table V-2. Rotation Characteristics, Nebraska

Tillage/Rotation	Soil Erosion (t/ac/yr)	Off-Farm Erosion Cost ($/ac/yr)[a]	Soil Depreciation ($/ac/yr)	Loss of Soil Carbon (t/ac/yr)	Carbon Loss Cost ($/ac/yr)[b]
Continuous Corn	6.5	4.5	8.7	0.11	4.3
Corn-Beans with					
Inorganic Inputs	3.7	2.6	3.2	0.13	5.4
Fertilizer Only	3.7	2.6	2.9	0.13	5.4
Organic Treatment	3.1	2.2	(2.3)	0.08	3.3
Corn-Beans-Corn					
Oats/Clover with					
Inorganic Inputs	3.1	2.2	(1.4)[b]	0.15	5.8
Fertilizer Only	3.1	2.2	(1.2)	0.15	5.8
Organic Treatment	2.2	1.6	(3.2)	0.10	4.0

a. Estimated using a damage cost of $0.72 per ton. Off-farm costs are weighted by crops and set-aside acreages that apply under FACTA.

b. Parentheses indicate appreciation in soil asset values due to increased productivity.

tial of these agricultural areas to serve as carbon sinks appears insignificant.

Policy Analysis

Every five years the basic enabling legislation for the U.S. farm programs is rewritten. This legislation, commonly referred to as the "farm bill," covers all aspects of agricultural pricing policy and farm-income support as well as agricultural trade, research, and numerous conservation provisions.

The commodity provisions of the farm bill provide income support to farmers who voluntarily participate in the programs. A "target price" for seven crop commodities is set by law to be used to determine the government's payment to farmers. On each unit of production of the seven "program crops," the government provides a "deficiency payment" equal to the difference between the market price and the target price.[3] In exchange for these payments, the farmer must limit program crop planting to the historical "base acreage." At the same time, part of the base acreage must be "set aside" in an "Acreage Conservation Reserve" as determined by the Department of Agriculture. Under the latest farm bill, FACTA, farmers cannot receive program payments on more than 85 percent of their base acreage, or for more than their "farm program payment yield," which is an average yield over a specified period.[4] The "normal flex acreage" is the 15 percent of base acreage on which farmers do not receive payments. On that land, they are allowed to plant any program crop, any oilseed (including soybeans), or any industrial or experimental crop (including adzuki, faba, lupin, and mung beans). Crops that may not be grown include any fruit, vegetable, tree or nut crop, peanuts, tobacco, or wild rice (U.S. Senate, 1990).

For the rotations examined, Table V-3 illustrates how these provisions affect what farmers plant. Taking a corn-beans rotation as an example, the table shows the percentage of base acreage that would be planted to corn, soybeans, etc.,

Table V-3. Plantings under Different Agricultural Programs and Crop Rotations (percent of total acreage).

Rotation	Food Security Act of 1985 (FSA)	Food, Agriculture, Conservation, and Trade Act of 1990 (FACTA)	Integrated Farm Management Program Option (IFM)	Dunkel Text (GATT)
Continuous Corn				
Corn	90	80	N.A.	82.5
ACR	10	5	N.A.	2.5
NFA	N.A.	15	N.A.	15
Corn-Beans				
Corn	45	40	N.A.	41.25
Soybeans	50	50	N.A.	50
ACR	5	2.5	N.A.	1.25
NFA	N.A.	7.5	N.A.	7.5
Corn-Beans-Corn-Oats/Clover				
Corn	45	40	40	41.25
Soybeans	25	25	25	25
Oats/Clover	25	21.25	21.25	21.25
ACR	5	2.5	2.5	1.25
NFA	N.A.	11.25	11.25	11.25
Alternative Cash Grain				
Corn	36	32	N.A.	33
Barley/Soybeans	18	16	N.A.	16.5
Wheat/Clover	19	16	N.A.	16.5
Soybeans	20	20	N.A.	20
ACR	7	4	N.A.	2
NFA	N.A.	12	N.A.	12
Alternative Cash Grain with Fodder				
Corn	18	16	16	16.5
Soybeans	20	20	20	20
Wheat/Clover	19	16	16	16.5
Clover	20	20	20	20
Corn Silage	20	20	20	20
ACR	3	2	2	1
NFA	N.A.	6	6	6

ACR = acreage conservation reserve ("set aside" acres); NFA = normal flex acres.

removed from production under the acreage conservation reserve, and put under the normal flex acres. Since soybeans are not considered a program crop, there are no base acres for soybeans, no acreage set-aside, and no normal flex acreage requirements. Half the farm would be used for soybean production.

Corn, however, is a program crop and subject to commodity programs provisions. The farmer in this case would be required to remove from production ("set-aside") 5 percent of the corn acreage (2.5 percent of the farm's planted acreage). The Department of Agriculture determines how much of each crop base must be set aside according to expectations of crop supply and price. Fifteen percent of the corn base (7.5 percent of the land) would be considered normal flex acres and could be planted to any of the crops listed above, including corn, which would be the choice under a corn-beans rotation. The farmer would receive government deficiency payments on corn for 80 percent of the corn base (40 percent of the land).

The other columns in Table V-3 show land use under other policy programs tested. The first was the Food Security Act of 1985 (FSA), FACTA's precursor. In terms of commodity provisions relevant to this discussion,[5] the FSA provided program payments on more acreage than the FACTA. The 1985 Act made no provision for the normal flex acres and the acreage, and some of its acreage conservation reserve requirements (notably for corn and wheat) were higher than the FACTA's.

One option allowed under the FACTA, "the Integrated Farm Management Program Option" (IFM), was intended to make it easier for farmers to convert to resource-conserving rotations. This option restricts eligibility to certain rotations that cut fertilizer and agrochemical use and to planting cover crops. The IFM's main advantage is allowing farmers to switch to alternative rotations while receiving prior program payments and maintaining crop base acreage.[6]

The last column of Table V-3 shows how the provisions of the "Dunkel Text" are interpreted.

The Dunkel Text is a negotiating text for the General Agreement on Tariffs and Trade (GATT) put forward by Arthur Dunkel, its director general. It differs from relevant U.S. farm programs mainly in its lower acreage set-aside requirements.

The original analysis for these two U.S. case studies (Faeth et al., 1991) was completed before passage of the 1990 Act (FACTA). The updated analysis was carried out to determine if commodity program changes encouraged or discouraged sustainable farming practices.

The procedures used in this analysis, and the crop rotations evaluated were identical to those used previously (Tables V-1 and V-2) and explained in the Technical Annex. Farm-level crop prices (Table V-4), target prices (Table V-5), and acreage conservation-reserve requirements were revised to reflect the latest projections for the United States (FAPRI, 1992). Additionally, production costs and off-farm costs were inflated.

The Farm Bills of 1985 and 1990 Net farm income for all rotations in both Nebraska and Pennsylvania was lower under FACTA (1990) than under FSA (1985).[7] *(See Annex Tables AV-1, AV-2, and AV-3.)* The profitability of alternative rotations also decreased more dramatically under FACTA in both case studies. As a result, in Pennsylvania during the transition period and in Nebraska, the gap between the profitability of conventional and alternative rotations widened. For the transition period (first five years) plus normal period (second five years) for Pennsylvania, alternative rotations remained the most profitable choice.

Over the long run, both alternative rotations have higher net operating incomes than the conventional rotations. Government payments (highest for the conventional rotations) skew this outcome so that the corn-beans rotation is ultimately more profitable than the alternative (low government support level).

The principal reasons for the lower net incomes and divergence between conventional and alternative rotations are:

Table V-4. Crop Prices[a,b]

Crop	FSA (1992–96)	FACTA IFM and Input Tax (1993–97)	Dunkel Text (1993–97)	Actual Under FACTA (1991)
Corn ($/bu)	2.05	2.30	2.37	2.37
Soybeans ($/bu)	5.80	5.82	6.05	5.60
Wheat ($/bu)	3.34	3.00	3.02	3.00
Barley ($/bu)	2.06	2.14	2.22	2.10
Oats ($/bu)	1.66	1.29	1.33	1.20
Alfalfa ($/mt)	85.00	77.37	77.37	—
Clover ($/mt)	85.00	72.09	72.09	—
Corn Silage[c]($/mt)	21.33	23.20	23.20	23.20

Table V-5. Target Prices ($/bu)

Crop	FSA	FACTA and Input Tax	Dunkel Text	IFM
Corn ($/bu)	2.75	2.75	2.75	2.75
Wheat ($/bu)	4.00	4.00	4.00	0.00
Barley ($/bu)	2.36	2.36	2.06	0.00
Oats ($/bu)	1.45	1.45	1.45	1.45

FSA = Food Security Act of 1985; FACTA = Food, Agriculture, Conservation and Trade Act of 1990; IFM = Integrated Farm Management Program Option

a. Prices from the Food and Agricultural Policy Research Institute publications: Dunkel prices from "Implications of a GATT Agreement for World Commodity Markets, 1993–1998: An Analysis of the Dunkel Text on Agriculture," FAPRI Staff Report #3-92, April 1992, pp 58–63. All other prices from "FAPRI 1992 U.S. Agriculture Outlook, " Staff Report #1-92, May 1992, pp 47, 49, 51, 53, 55, 57, 61.

b. We have not included in this analysis a price differential between conventionally and organically grown products, even though a price differential does exist. Organically grown products can command a price up to 20 percent greater than that for conventionally grown products. (Ron Tammen, pers. comm., July 27, 1990.)

c. Price for corn silage is determined locally as this crop cannot be transported economically over long distances. The latest state price (1991) from the Pennsylvania Agricultural Statistics Service was used for 1993–1997.

- the change in actual and projected farm-level prices, with significant increases, particularly for corn, and significant decreases for wheat, oats, and clover *(Table V-3)*;

- a decrease in the acreage eligible for government payments because of the normal flex acres;

- an increase in production costs due to inflation (while target prices remained constant).

Net economic values for most alternative rotations declined for FACTA relative to FSA while the net economic values for conventional practices increased *(Figures V-1 to V-9, Annex Tables AV-4, AV-5, and AV-6)*. These results were due primarily to the strong farm-level corn price and weak farm-level prices for barley, oats, and wheat, the crops used in alternative rotations.

Agrochemical tax As an adjunct to the policy analysis for FSA and FACTA, the impact of an agrochemical tax on the selection of the most financially profitable production systems was examined. An agrochemical tax is used to signal environmental damage, such as groundwater contamination caused by overuse. Under this scenario, baseline policy (FACTA) remained unaltered. For both case studies, sensitivity analysis was done to see at what point taxation would equalize net farm income under the most financially profitable alternative system and under the most profitable conventional system.

In Nebraska, the required agrochemical tax rate was 33 percent, much higher than the 12 percent tax rate in Faeth et al. (1991). This result again demonstrates the divergence in profitability of the alternative and conventional systems under FACTA. In Pennsylvania, an agrochemical tax rate of 50 percent during the transition period was required before net farm income of an alternative rotation exceeded the net farm income of the most profitable conventional rotation. This was much larger than the 16-percent tax rate needed in the previous analysis. No tax was required in either study for the transition plus nor-

mal period, since an alternative rotation is already most profitable.

Integrated Farm Management Program Option
This program option was originally submitted as the Sustainable Agriculture Adjustment Act of 1989 and passed as the IFM option of the 1990 Farm Act. IFM was intended to give farmers a way to switch to alternative rotations while maintaining their farm program payment revenue.

To participate in the IFM program, producers must develop and implement an integrated farm management plan that improves the soil and protects surface and groundwater supplies by minimizing agricultural pollutants. At least 20 percent of all crop acreage bases on the farm must be planted to resource-conserving crops.[8]

This program has often been misunderstood. Producers participating in this program do *not* lose crop acreage base when they plant base acres to resource-conserving crops. Program payment yields will *not* be reduced when producers make the transition to a new cropping system, even if crop yields temporarily decline. Producers receive deficiency payments on program crop acreage planted to resource-conserving crops (Langley, 1992a).

The language of the 1990 Farm Act indicates that producers could harvest and sell small-grain crops, except malting barley and wheat, as grain (as opposed to seed), on all acreage devoted to resource-conserving crops as part of an approved IFM plan. Producers could also receive the deficiency payment for the original participating program crop on all such acreage.

Confusion has surrounded IFM since its enactment. Regulations were not completed until the week before farmers were to sign up, few USDA staffers seem to know much about the program, and the USDA restricted enrollment to one million acres per year (Langley, 1992a), when Congress intended an enrollment of 5 million acres per year (U.S. House of Representatives, 1990). As a result of the confusion and these restrictions, only 55,000 acres were enrolled in the first year of the program, and only 40,000 acres the second year (Langley, 1992b).

The USDA Agricultural Stabilization and Conservation Service (ASCS) has interpreted the IFM Program Option in a way that prohibits producers from harvesting specific program commodities from any acreage devoted to resource-conserving crops (Langley, 1992c) and selling those small-grain crops (i.e., oats and nonmalting barley) as grain. The language of the IFM Program Option of the 1990 farm bill, however, does not specifically proscribe harvesting and selling oats or nonmalting barley on land that is not "set-aside" (U.S. Senate 1990; Sustainable Agriculture Working Group, 1991, 1992).

To determine what effect the intended Act and the USDA interpretation of the Act have on producer's decisions financially, economically, and environmentally, both the language and the USDA interpretation of the IFM Program Option were analyzed.[9] In Nebraska, under the IFM program as intended by the United States Congress, the net farm income of IFM-participating rotations exceeded that under FACTA by $60 to $62 per acre over the four-year rotation *(Figure V-8, Annex Table AV-3)*. However, even the increase in net farm income for rotations participating in the IFM program did not alter the profitability ranking of rotations.

Using the USDA interpretation of the IFM program in Nebraska, the net farm income of IFM-participating rotations decreased between $9 and $12 per acre over the four-year rotation relative to their baseline counterparts. Net farm income decreased for IFM-participating rotations because producers complying with the USDA interpretation of the policy could neither harvest nor sell the oats if they wanted to receive the deficiency payments for the original program crop.

Dunkel Text Under the Dunkel policy scenario, changes in agricultural policy would occur in three areas: export competition, internal support, and market access (FAPRI, 1992). Export competition, defined as subsidy expenditures and subsidized export commodities, is to be reduced be-

tween 24 percent and 36 percent from 1986–90 levels. Internal support of agricultural commodities (the difference between average domestic price and lower world prices) is to be reduced 20 percent from 1986–88 average levels. Market access restrictions are transformed into tariffs and reduced by 5 percent each year for seven years starting in 1993 (Jurenas, 1992).

The United States would receive credit for policy changes since 1986 so that the wheat, feed grain, cotton, soybean, and rice programs would be in compliance without any modifications (FAPRI, 1992). Only slight modifications would be needed in the U.S. cane sugar and milk programs.

Two major changes are assumed for the Dunkel scenario. World and U.S. prices for wheat, feed grains, and soybeans would increase *(Table V-4)* and the acreage conservation reserve for program commodities would decrease *(Table V-3, column 5)*. Target prices would not change.

Incorporating the impacts of the Dunkel proposal into the analysis raised net farm income of all rotations in Pennsylvania and Nebraska over FACTA values. The respective rankings for net farm income and net economic value would not change under the proposal.

Decoupling Alternative

The 1990 legislation thus presents considerable obstacles to producers who want to adopt sustainable farming practices. Although the social value is greater for the alternative rotations than for the conventional practices in areas where resource costs are high, such as Pennsylvania, the structure of financial incentives under the commodity programs discourages their adoption. The basic flaw in U.S. farm income support programs is their tie to commodity production. This tie distorts farmers' production decisions and makes the support programs a regressive and inefficient means of improving rural welfare.

What difference would restructuring farm support programs make? A final illustrative scenario assumes that government support payments are not based on commodity production but on the amount required to equalize net income for each rotation. Payments were calculated to bring income to the level of the best conventional rotation in each case. *(See Tables V-6 and V-7.)*

In Pennsylvania, corn-beans under conventional tillage is the most profitable rotation under FACTA during the transition period. Payments would have to be made on every other rotation to make net income equal to that of corn-beans in the transition period. However, savings could be realized in terms of gains in net economic value for the alternative rotations, particularly those using reduced tillage. For example, an additional payment of $90 over five years for the alternative cash grain with fodder system using reduced tillage would result in an economic gain of $107 over the same period.

Table V-6. Gains from Decoupling, Pennsylvania

	Transition Period ($/acre/5 yr)							
	Conventional Tillage				**Reduced Tillage**			
	CC	**CCBCB**	**ACG**	**ACGF**	**CC**	**CCBCB**	**ACG**	**ACGF**
FACTA NFI	12	247	154	152	(2)	237	155	157
Saving[a]	(235)	—	(93)	(95)	(249)	(10)	(92)	(90)
FACTA NEV	(526)	(102)	(106)	(34)	(450)	(78)	(72)	5
Gain in NEV[b]	(424)	—	(4)	68	(348)	24	30	107
	Normal Period ($/acre/5 yr)							
FACTA NFI	212	486	631	550	213	476	632	553
Savings	(274)	—	145	64	(273)	(10)	146	67
FACTA NEV	(310)	137	359	353	(235)	160	392	292
Gain in NEV	(447)	—	222	216	(372)	23	255	255

CC = Continuous conventional corn, herbicide and inorganic fertilizer use; CCBCB = Conventional corn-soybean rotation, herbicide and inorganic fertilizer use; ACG = Alternative cash grain, corn-corn-soybean wheat/clover-barley, organic production with mechanical weed control and green manure plowdown; ACGF = Alternative cash grain with fodder production, corn-soybean-wheat/clover-clover-corn silage, organic production with mechanical weed control and animal manure plowdown.

a. Savings is the decrease (or increase) in direct income support that is required for the net farm income of each rotation to equal that of the most profitable conventional rotation (CCBCB) under current policy. ($NFI_{ROTATION} - NFI_{CCBCB} = Savings_{ROTATION}$).
b. Gain in Net Economic Value represents the possible savings (or loss) to society if producers switched from the predominant practice (CCBCB) to an alternative rotation under current policy. ($NEV_{ROTATION} - NEV_{CCBCB} = Gain \ in \ NEV_{ROTATION}$).

Table V-7. Gains from Decoupling, Nebraska

				($/acre/4 yr)			
	CC	**HFCB**	**FOCB**	**ORGCB**	**HFROT**	**FOROT**	**ORGROT**
FACTA NFI	228	567	**571**	561	405	402	398
Savings[a]	(343)	(4)	—	(10)	(166)	(169)	(173)
FACTA NEV	114	509	**512**	504	342	339	337
Gain in NEV[b]	(398)	(3)	—	(8)	(170)	(173)	(175)

CC = Conventional continuous corn with herbicide and inorganic fertilizer use; HFCB = Conventional corn-soybean rotation with herbicide and inorganic fertilizer use; FOCB = Corn-soybean rotation with inorganic fertilizer use only, no herbicides; ORGCB = Corn-soybean rotation with no herbicide or inorganic fertilizer use, animal manure applied during the corn year; HFROT = Corn-soybean-corn-oats/clover, herbicides and inorganic fertilizer use; FOROT = Corn-soybean-corn-oats/clover, inorganic fertilizer use but no herbicides; ORGROT = Corn-soybean-corn-oats/clover, organic rotation with manure application.

a. Savings represents the decrease or (increase) in direct income support that is required for the Net Farm Income of each rotation to equal that of the most profitable conventional rotation (FOCB) under baseline policy. $(NFI_{ROTATION} - NFI_{FOCB} = Savings_{ROTATION})$

b. Gain in Net Economic Value represents the possible economic savings or (loss) to society if producers switched from the predominant practice (FOCB) to an alternative rotation under current policy. $(NEV_{ROTATION} - NEV_{FOCB} = GAIN \text{ in } NEV_{ROTATION})$

This saving would be amplified in following years. Helping farmers to get through the financially difficult transition period would realize large future savings. Incomes could be maintained with lower government payments and large gains in net economic value. For the same alternative rotation, payments could be reduced by $67 over five years, farm income would be the same as it is under the best conventional rotation, and society would gain $255 in net economic value.

In Nebraska, because the resource costs associated with the various production practices are small, farmers already use practices that have the largest net economic value. Abandoning them for others would result in no gain in net economic value. Though only illustrative, these results do show that restructuring farm programs could bring about significant fiscal and economic improvement.

Conclusions

For over sixty years, U.S. government intervention in the agricultural sector has entailed significant fiscal costs and led to chronic surpluses. The economic distortions caused by these interventions have engendered ever more intervention and made programs ever more complex. Many farmers today are "farming the programs" and are unable to make sound production decisions based on market signals and resource efficiency.

The changes in the commodity support provisions of the 1990 Farm Bill have moved the country toward a greater free-market orientation, but not necessarily toward greater sustainability. Taken as a whole, agricultural policy in the United States is still inherently biased against resource-conserving production systems. Provisions such as "normal flex acres," give farmers some flexibility, but most planted acreage still remains subject to the restrictions of the commodity programs. Limits on farm program payment yields may encourage farmers to base decisions about inputs on market prices—a positive step. But, at the same time, "acreage conservation reserve" provisions encourage farmers to take lowest yielding land out of production and to intensify production on the rest. Conservation compliance provisions require farmers to put highly erodible land under a conservation plan, but only program crops will be subsidized, and those may not be optimal from a conservation standpoint. Further, the way provisions such as the Integrated Farm Management Program Option have been interpreted and implemented actually reduces participating farmers' income.

These disadvantages are great. Nevertheless, where resource costs are high—as they are in Pennsylvania, for instance—alternative practices can pay off over the long run. The resource costs of the alternatives are lower and inherent profitability higher. But farmers must first survive the difficult transition period. Even where resource costs are low—as they are in Nebraska—alternative practices can be competitive with conventional practices.

The challenge to agricultural policy-makers will be to create consistent incentives for all farmers to take up practices that are in line with what is most economical for society.

The challenge to agricultural policy-makers will be to create consistent incentives for all farmers to take up practices that are in line with what is most economical for society. As the Pennsylvania case study shows, government payments can be inversely proportional to the environmen-tal damage they cause. Commodity program-caused distortions like these must be removed.

Although their champions claim that farm income-support payments support "family farming," most farm program benefits do not go to small, low-income producers. In fact, most go to large commercial farmers. Direct income-support programs should not be tied to commodity production but to financial need and the use of sound management practices. Means-tests and lower payment limitations should be applied to target available agricultural support funds to the farmers who need the help.

The aspects of farm income support outlined in the Dunkel Text reflect political reality but do not go far enough to ensure sustainability. Structural adjustments worldwide would be eased if the European Community and Japan, co-operating with the United States, also reduced their large producer subsidies, opened their agricultural markets, and stopped dumping surplus production on world markets. These changes would lighten the burden on their own taxpayers and consumers, and the resulting increase in world commodity prices would boost incomes for U.S. farmers and reduce the fiscal costs of federal income-support programs. Furthermore, bringing these changes about need not interfere with efforts to maintain or strengthen environmental and phytosanitary standards.

At home, U.S. agriculture's exemption from the "polluter pays principle" should be dropped. Farmers should pay fines and fees for their off-site pollution just as mining and construction industries do; instead, they are offered federal cost-sharing for conservation activities. If farmers had to pay the pollution costs of their inputs, they would need little encouragement to switch to practices that conserve soil and water, to reduce off-site damages, and to employ cost-reducing biological means of managing soil fertility and pests. Any revenue collected as pollution penalties should be earmarked for agricultural research to help farmers reduce their reliance on pesticides and fertilizers. Several states already have programs that channel funds in this way.

Figure V-1. Net Economic Value, Pennsylvania Case Study, Full 10-Year Period Using Conventional Tillage

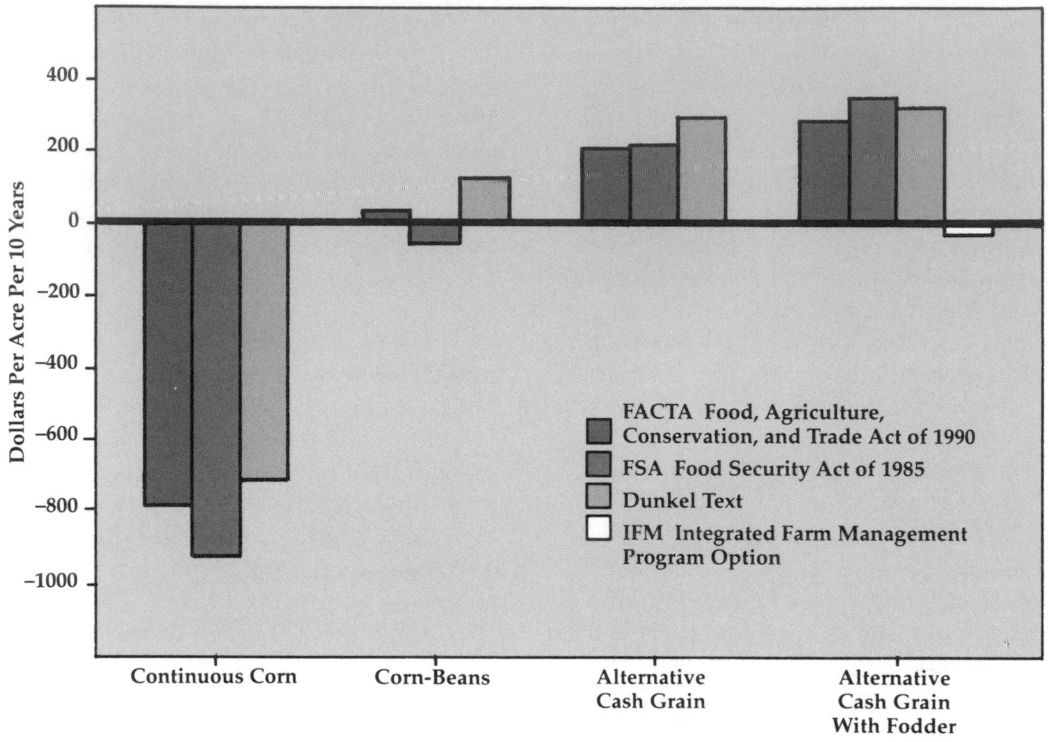

Source: Data from this report

Figure V-2. Net Farm Income, Pennsylvania Case Study, Full 10-Year Period Using Conventional Tillage

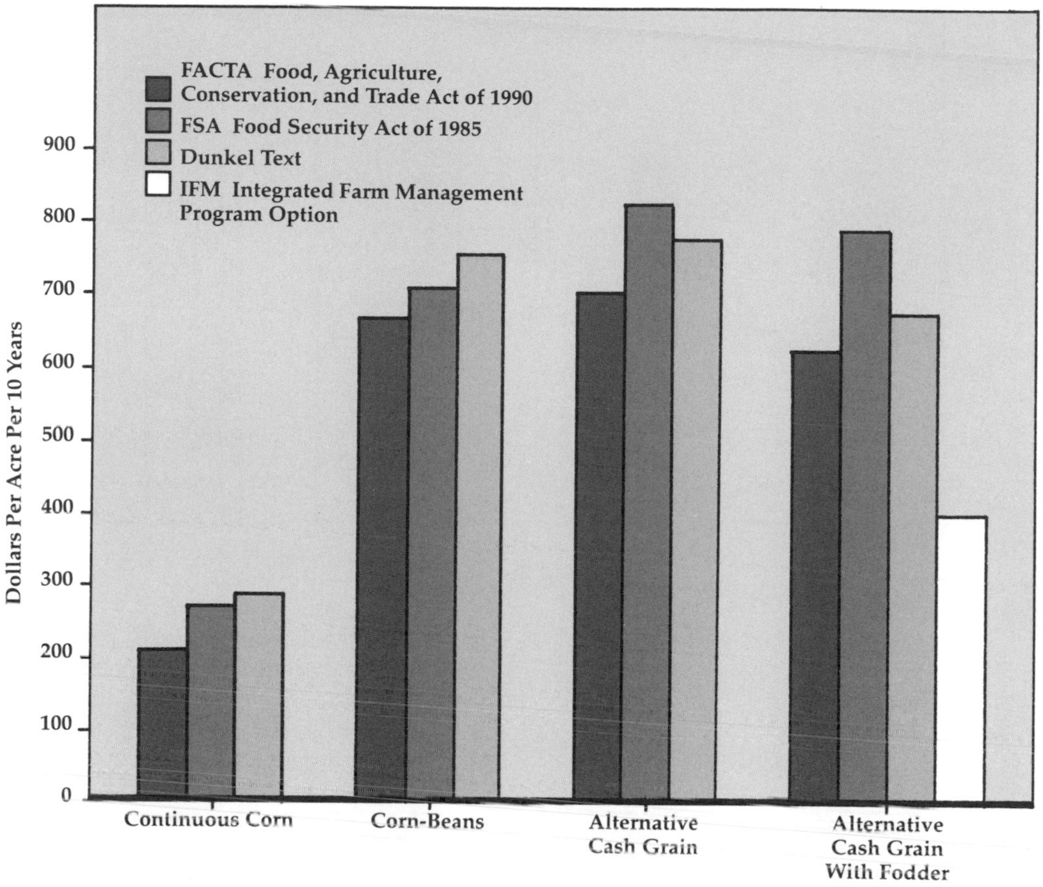

Source: Data from this report

Figure V-3. Net Farm Operating Income*, Pennsylvania Case Study, Full 10-Year Period Using Conventional Tillage

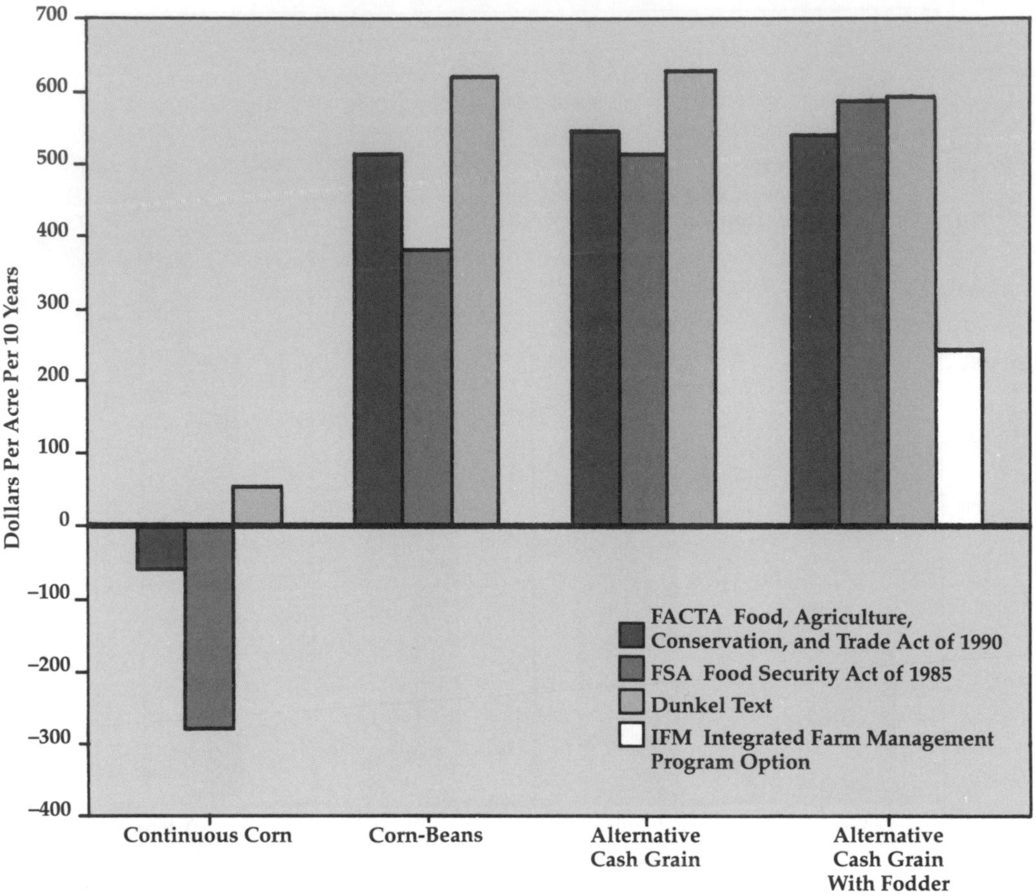

700
600
500
400
300
200
100
0
–100
–200
–300
–400
Dollars Per Acre Per 10 Years
FACTA Food, Agriculture, Conservation, and Trade Act of 1990
FSA Food Security Act of 1985
Dunkel Text
IFM Integrated Farm Management Program Option
Continuous Corn
Corn-Beans
Alternative Cash Grain
Alternative Cash Grain With Fodder

*Net Farm Income Before Subsidies

Source: Data from this report

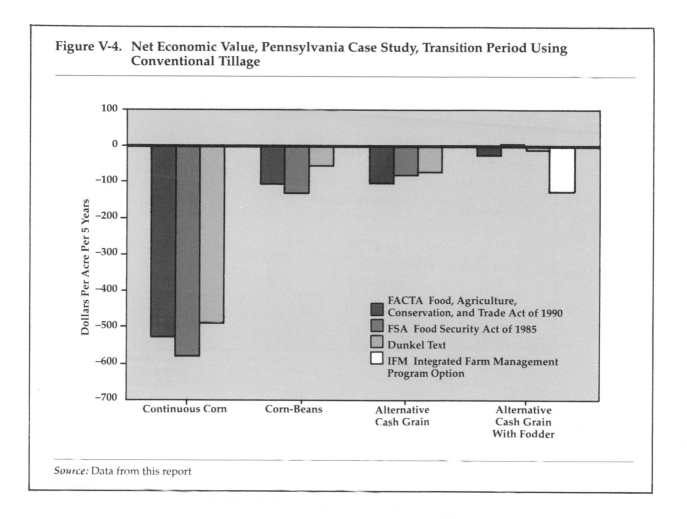

Figure V-4. Net Economic Value, Pennsylvania Case Study, Transition Period Using Conventional Tillage

FACTA Food, Agriculture, Conservation, and Trade Act of 1990
FSA Food Security Act of 1985
Dunkel Text
IFM Integrated Farm Management Program Option

Source: Data from this report

Figure V-5. Net Farm Income, Pennsylvania Case Study, Transition Period Using Conventional Tillage

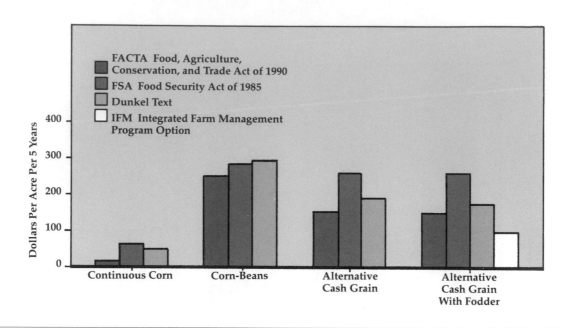

Source: Data from this report

80

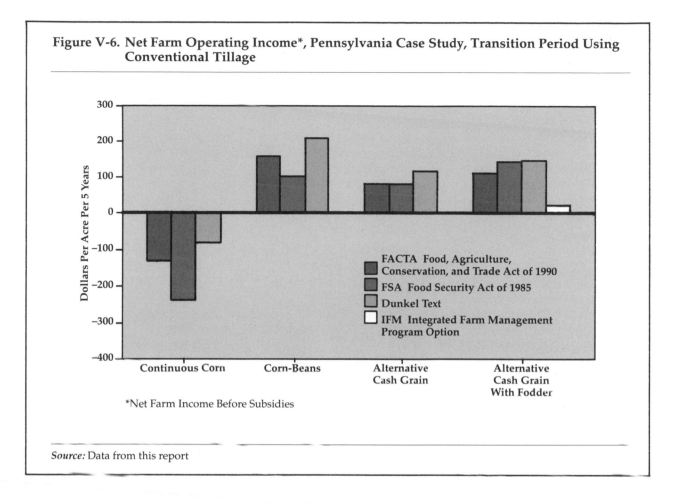

Figure V-6. Net Farm Operating Income*, Pennsylvania Case Study, Transition Period Using Conventional Tillage

*Net Farm Income Before Subsidies

Source: Data from this report

Figure V-7. Net Economic Value, Nebraska Case Study

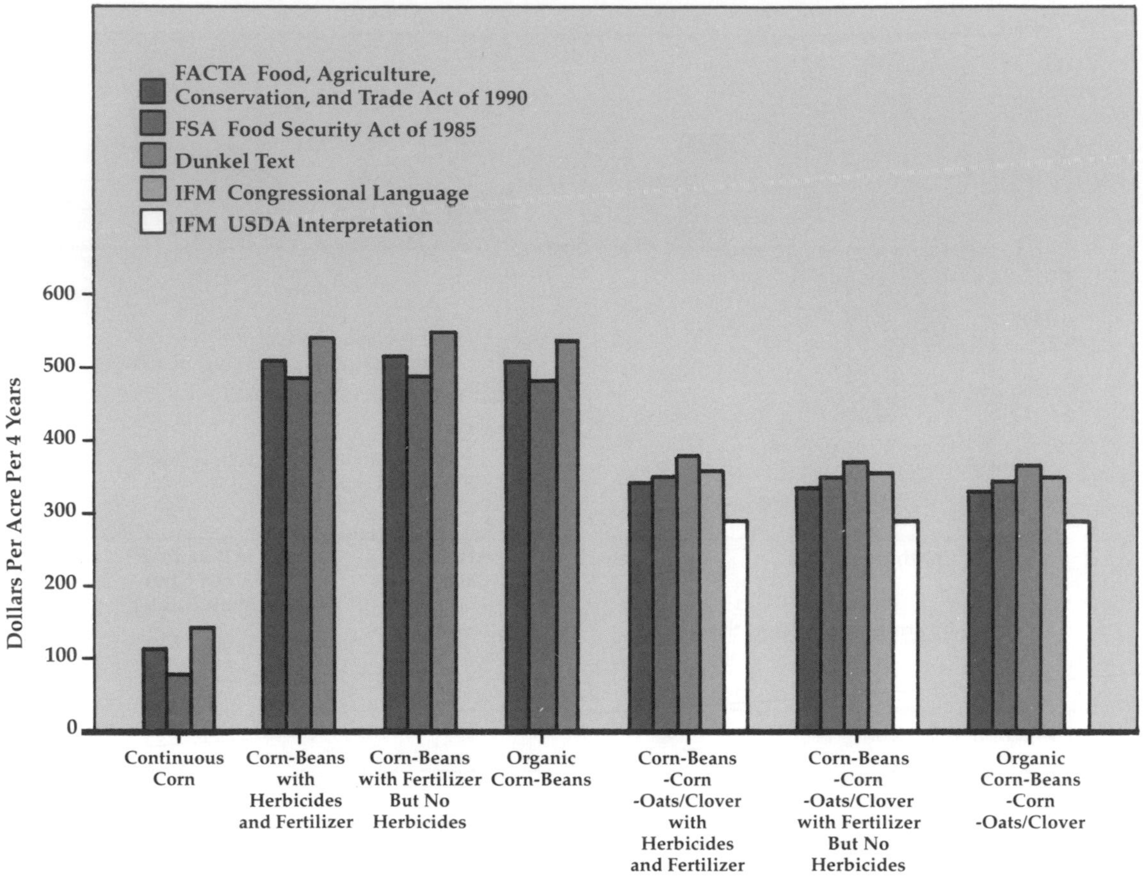

FACTA Food, Agriculture, Conservation, and Trade Act of 1990
FSA Food Security Act of 1985
Dunkel Text
IFM Congressional Language
IFM USDA Interpretation
Dollars Per Acre Per 4 Years
600
500
400
300
200
100
0
Continuous Corn
Corn-Beans with Herbicides and Fertilizer
Corn-Beans with Fertilizer But No Herbicides
Organic Corn-Beans
Corn-Beans -Corn -Oats/Clover with Herbicides and Fertilizer
Corn-Beans -Corn -Oats/Clover with Fertilizer But No Herbicides
Organic Corn-Beans -Corn -Oats/Clover

Source: Data from this report

Figure V-8. Net Farm Income, Nebraska Case Study

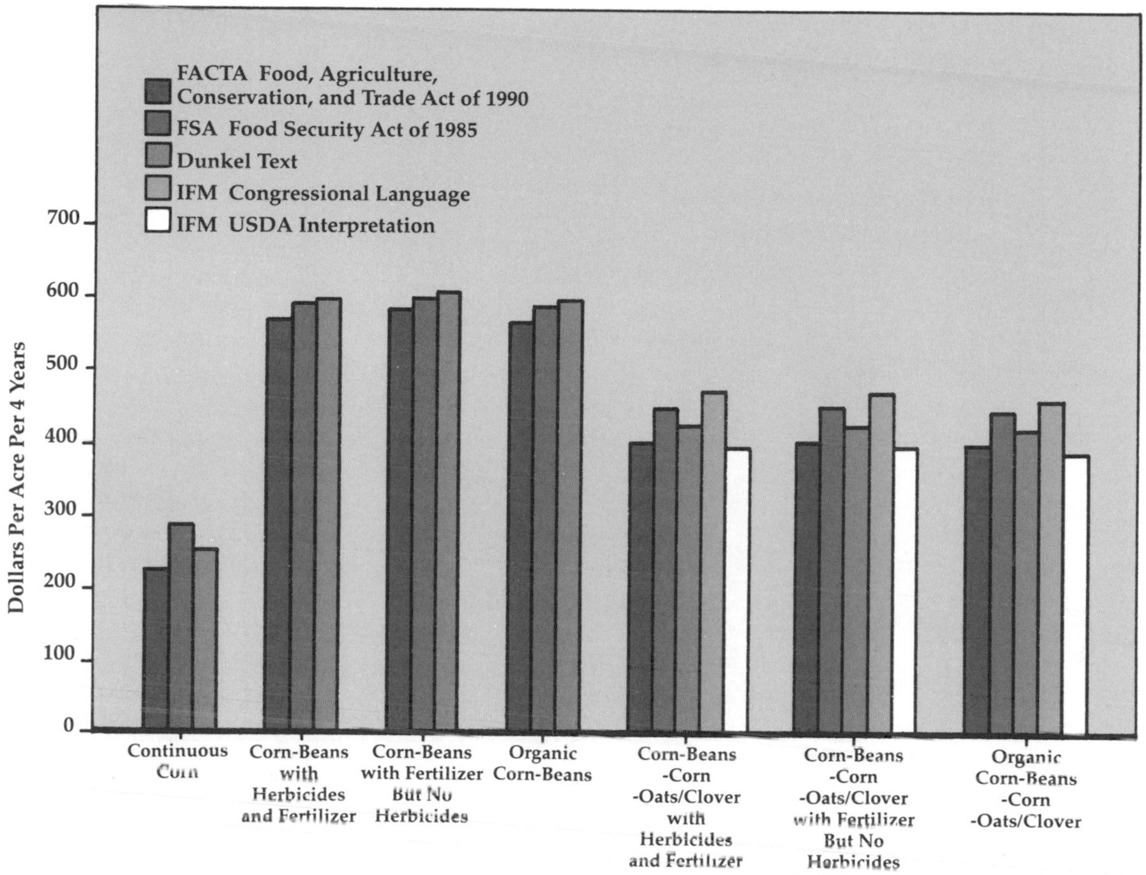
FACTA Food, Agriculture, Conservation, and Trade Act of 1990
FSA Food Security Act of 1985
Dunkel Text
IFM Congressional Language
IFM USDA Interpretation
Dollars Per Acre Per 4 Years
700
600
500
400
300
200
100
0
Continuous Corn
Corn-Beans with Herbicides and Fertilizer
Corn-Beans with Fertilizer But No Herbicides
Organic Corn-Beans
Corn-Beans -Corn -Oats/Clover with Herbicides and Fertilizer
Corn-Beans -Corn -Oats/Clover with Fertilizer But No Herbicides
Organic Corn-Beans -Corn -Oats/Clover

Source: Data from this report

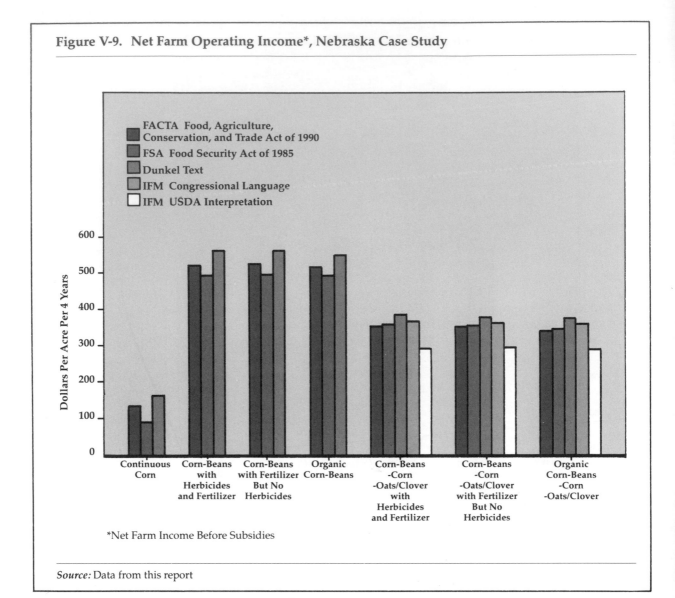

Figure V-9. Net Farm Operating Income*, Nebraska Case Study

FACTA Food, Agriculture, Conservation, and Trade Act of 1990
FSA Food Security Act of 1985
Dunkel Text
IFM Congressional Language
IFM USDA Interpretation

*Net Farm Income Before Subsidies

Source: Data from this report

Current U.S. farm income-support programs are inefficient and regressive. They need a major overhaul to reduce fiscal outlays, to equitably redistribute government income support, and to develop and bring into use technologies that take a lighter toll on the environment. Policy should act as an incentive, not a deterrent, to sustainable natural resource use.

Notes

1. By law, farmers may receive government payments only if they grow one of the following crops: feedgrains (corn, sorghum), wheat, barley, oats, rice, and cotton.

2. Reilly and Richards (1992) have provided similar estimates based on potential economic welfare losses from global warming's effects on forests, water resources, fisheries, coastal areas, population migration and resettlement, agriculture, etc.

3. If the market price is greater than the target price, no payment is made.

4. At the Secretary of Agriculture's discretion, the farm program payment yield may be (a) the actual yield or (b) the average yield for the five years preceding 1986, excluding the highest and lowest yields. The practice, (b) has been used, effectively freezing farm program payment yields at their 1986 level.

5. The cropland considered in these case studies is not "highly-erodible" and so conservation compliance provisions do not apply.

6. Crop base acres are a running average of the last five years' plantings. Farmers who plant crops for which they have no base lose base for crops for which they do have an established base. For example, if a farmer with an established base for corn of 100 acres were to plant clover for one year, the corn base would be reduced to 80 acres in the following year and program payments would be similarly reduced commensurately.

7. FSA results are reported in 1990 dollars; the results for other policy tests, in 1993 dollars. To have inflated the FSA target prices, market prices, costs of production, and off-site costs would have made the FSA results reported here inconsistent with those reported in Faeth et al. (1991). The principal conclusions noted here, however, would not have changed.

8. Resource-conserving crops include: legumes grown as forage or green manure (such as clover or alfalfa); legume-grass mixtures (grasses being perennial grasses used for haying or grazing); legume-small grain mixtures (any small grain but malting barley or wheat, except wheat interplanted with other small-grain crops for nonhuman consumption); legume-grass-small grain mixtures; and alternative crops (soil- and water-conserving experimental or industrial crops grown in arid and semiarid regions) (Langley 1992a).

9 In the analysis of the Integrated Farm Management Program Option, the assumption was that producers changed from a continuous corn production system (in which they participated in the commodity programs) to one of the alternative rotations that met the requirements of this provision. In Nebraska, three different treatments of one rotation qualified (HFROT, FOROT, ORGROT). One rotation, with conventional and reduced tillage, qualified in Pennsylvania (ACGF).

Technical Annex V

Methodology Update—Nebraska and Pennsylvania Case Studies

Estimates of environmental costs were based on detailed physical, agronomic, and economic modeling of soil, water, and chemical transport from the field and their implications for water quality and soil fertility. Data from nine years of field experiments at the Rodale Research Center in Kutztown, Pennsylvania and at the University of Nebraska Research Station at Mead *(Box V-1)* were analyzed using the U.S. Department of Agriculture (USDA) Erosion-Productivity Impact Calculator (EPIC) Model (Williams et al., 1989).

On- and Off-Farm Costs

Output from EPIC was used to estimate the on- and off-farm soil costs associated with conventional and alternative crop rotations. Other problems associated with agricultural production, such as groundwater contamination, loss of wildlife habitat, soil salinization or toxic buildups, or human health problems due to the use of toxics, were not addressed. Hydrological models, for example, were inadequate, so economic losses associated with groundwater contamination could not be determined. The nature of the case study approach ruled out exploration of large-scale trade-offs in surface water quality, soil erosion, and groundwater quality, in which benefits in one area may be offset by costs in another as land use changes (Hrubovcak et al., 1990).

Methodology, Estimating Soil Depreciation Allowances

The yield change for each rotation period was taken to be the total yield change for the 30-year simulation *divided by* the number of rotations in 30 years, thereby assuming a linear change in yields. In this way, the productivity change for each rotation included only the change attributable to the rotation over one rotation period. Since input costs were invariant in relation to yields, this change in yields was multiplied by

the crop price to determine the loss in net farm income for the period. The present value of all income losses over the next 30 years, using a 5-percent real (excluding inflation) discount rate, represents the loss in soil asset value. Technology was held constant. A "normal" weather year was used for each of the 30 annual simulations, thereby eliminating the variability induced from random weather.

The formula used to determine the soil depreciation allowance was:

Soil Depreciation Allowance =

$$[(Y_o - Y_n)/(n/RL)] * P_c * \{[1 - 1/(1+i)n]/i\},$$

where Y_o is initial yield,
Y_n is final yield,
RL   is rotation length,
n   is period under consideration,
P_c is crop price, and
i   is real interest rate.

For rotations that include more than one crop, each crop was weighted according to its acreage in the rotation. When comparing rotations of different length, the rotation with the longest period was used to calculate the depreciation allowance for all rotations. The soil depreciation values are shown in Tables V-3 and V-4, column 3.

Payment Formula

For each program crop the payment formula is as follows:

$$(P_t - P_m) * AB * (1 - ACR - NFA) * PPY,$$

where P_t is the target price;

P_m is the market price;

AB is the acreage base for the crop;

ACR is the acreage conservation reserve fraction for the crop;

NFA is the normal flex acres, equal to 0.15, and

PPY is the Program Payment Yield.

Annex Table AV-1. Summary Results, Net Farm Income, Transition Period, Pennsylvania

Net Farm Income
($/ac/5 yr)

	Policy	Conventional Tillage				Reduced Tillage				
		CC	CCBCB	ACG	ACGF	CC	CCBCB	ACG	ACGF	ALLHAY
Gross	FACTA	8	293	64	68	(8)	279	61	63	(21)
Margin	FSA	(108)	226	61	92	(123)	212	58	88	54
	IFM	—	—	—	(27)	—	—	—	(31)	—
	50% Tax	(130)	198	64	68	(146)	184	61	63	(21)
	Dunkel	65	350	102	91	49	336	98	87	(21)
Minus	FACTA	139	131	(14)	(42)	137	127	(18)	(51)	20
Soil	FSA	124	123	(14)	(42)	122	119	(18)	(51)	(24)
Depre-	IFM	—	—	—	(42)	—	—	—	(51)	—
ciation	50% Tax	139	131	(14)	(42)	137	127	(18)	(51)	20
	Dunkel	143	135	(14)	(43)	141	131	(18)	(52)	20
Net	FACTA	(131)	162	78	110	(145)	152	79	114	(0)
Operating	FSA	(232)	103	75	134	(245)	93	76	139	78
Income	IFM	—	—	—	16	—	—	—	20	—
	50% Tax	(268)	67	78	110	(282)	57	79	114	(0)
	Dunkel	(78)	215	115	135	(92)	205	117	139	(0)
Plus	FACTA	142	85	76	42	142	85	76	42	0
Govern-	FSA	293	176	182	123	293	176	182	123	0
ment	IFM	—	—	—	84	—	—	—	84	—
	50% Tax	142	85	76	42	142	85	76	42	0
	Dunkel	124	74	66	37	124	74	66	37	0
Net	FACTA	12	247	154	152	(2)	237	155	157	0
Farm	FSA	61	279	257	257	48	269	258	262	78
Income	IFM	—	—	—	99	—	—	—	103	—
	50% Tax	(126)	152	154	152	(140)	142	155	157	0
	Dunkel	46	289	181	172	32	279	182	176	0

— = not applicable.

CC = continuous conventional corn; CCBCB = conventional corn-soybean rotation; ACG = alternative cash grain; ACGF = alternative cash grain with fodder; ALLHAY = continuous alfalfa production. *See* Note 7.

Annex Table AV-2. Summary Results, Transition and Normal Period, plus Present Value of Net Farm Income

Net Farm Income
($/ac/10 years)

| | Policy | Conventional Tillage | | | | Reduced Tillage | | | | |
		CC	CCBCB	ACG	ACGF	CC	CCBCB	ACG	ACGF	ALLHAY
Gross	FACTA	202	753	522	462	172	727	515	453	95
Margin	FSA	(47)	607	486	508	(75)	581	480	501	247
	IFM	—	—	—	165	—	—	—	156	—
	50% Tax	(55)	576	522	462	(85)	550	515	453	95
	Dunkel	318	869	610	510	288	843	603	502	95
Minus	FACTA	259	244	(25)	(79)	255	237	(34)	(95)	(38)
Soil	FSA	231	230	(26)	(78)	228	222	(34)	(95)	(45)
Depre-	IFM	—	—	—	(79)	—	—	—	(95)	—
ciation	50% Tax	259	244	(25)	(79)	255	237	(34)	(95)	(38)
	Dunkel	267	252	(26)	(80)	263	245	(34)	(97)	(38)
Net Oper-	FACTA	(57)	509	547	541	(83)	490	549	548	133
ating	FSA	(278)	377	512	587	(302)	359	514	596	292
Income	IFM	—	—	—	244	—	—	—	251	—
	50% Tax	(314)	332	547	541	(340)	313	549	548	133
	Dunkel	51	617	635	591	25	598	638	599	133
Plus	FACTA	265	159	153	87	265	159	153	87	0
Govern-	FSA	547	328	315	192	547	328	315	192	0
ment	IFM	—	—	—	156	—	—	—	156	—
Payments	50% Tax	265	159	153	87	265	159	153	87	0
	Dunkel	231	139	135	80	231	139	135	80	0
Net Farm	FACTA	208	668	700	628	182	649	702	635	133
Income	FSA	269	706	827	779	244	687	829	788	292
	IFM	—	—	—	400	—	—	—	407	—
	50% Tax	(49)	491	700	628	(75)	472	702	635	133
	Dunkel	283	756	770	671	256	737	773	680	133

— = not applicable.

CC = continuous conventional corn; CCBCB = conventional corn-soybean rotation; ACG = alternative cash grain; ACGF = alternative cash grain with fodder; ALLHAY = continuous alfalfa production. *See* Note 7.

Annex Table AV-3. Summary Results, Net Farm Income, Nebraska

Net Farm Income

($/ac/4 yr)

	Policy	CC	HFCB	FOCB	ORGCB	HFROT	FOROT	ORGROT
					Rotation			
Gross	FACTA	166	531	534	503	345	343	331
Margin	FSA	119	501	503	473	351	348	334
	33% Tax	114	508	524	503	319	326	331
	IFM-Cong	—	—	—	—	362	359	346
	IFM-USDA	—	—	—	—	287	288	277
	Dunkel	198	570	572	539	376	373	359
Minus	FACTA	35	13	11	(9)	(6)	(5)	(13)
Soil	FSA	31	12	11	(8)	(5)	(4)	(12)
Depre-	33% Tax	35	13	11	(9)	(6)	(5)	(13)
ciation	IFM-Cong	—	—	—	(9)	(6)	(5)	(13)
	IFM-USDA	—	—	—	(9)	(6)	(5)	(13)
	Dunkel	36	13	12	(10)	(6)	(5)	(13)
Net	FACTA	132	519	523	513	351	348	344
Operating	FSA	88	489	492	482	356	352	346
Income	33% Tax	79	495	512	513	324	331	344
	IFM-Cong	—	—	—	—	367	364	359
	IFM-USDA	—	—	—	—	293	293	289
	Dunkel	162	557	560	549	382	378	373
Plus	FACTA	97	48	48	48	54	54	54
Government	FSA	199	100	100	100	100	100	100
Payments	33% Tax	97	48	48	48	54	54	54
	IFM-Cong	—	—	—	—	100	100	100
	IFM-USDA	—	—	—	—	100	100	100
	Dunkel	84	42	42	42	46	46	46
Net Farm	FACTA	228	567	571	561	405	402	398
Income	FSA	287	589	592	581	455	451	445
	33% Tax	176	543	561	561	378	385	398
	IFM-Cong	—	—	—	—	467	463	458
	IFM-USDA	—	—	—	—	392	392	389
	Dunkel	247	599	602	591	428	424	419

— = not applicable.

CC = conventional continuous corn; HFCB = conventional corn-beans, w/herbicides and fertilizer; FOCB = corn-beans w/fertilizer but no herbicides; ORGCB = organic corn-beans; HFROT = corn-beans-corn-oats/clover with herbicides and fertilizer; FOROT = corn-bean-corn-oats/clover with fertilizer but no herbicides; ORGROT = organic corn-beans-corn-oats/clover.
See Note 7.

Annex Table AV-4. Summary Results - Net Economic Value, Transition Period, Pennsylvania

Net Economic Value
($/ac/5 yr)

	Policy	Conventional Tillage				Reduced Tillage				
		CC	CCBCB	ACG	ACGF	CC	CCBCB	ACG	ACGF	ALLHAY
Gross	FACTA	8	293	64	68	(8)	279	61	63	(21)
Margin	FSA	(108)	225	61	92	(123)	212	58	88	54
	IFM	—	—	—	(27)	—	—	—	(31)	—
	50% Tax	(130)	198	64	68	(146)	184	61	63	(21)
	Dunkel	65	350	102	91	49	336	98	87	(21)
Minus	FACTA	139	131	(14)	(42)	137	127	(18)	(51)	(20)
Soil	FSA	124	123	(14)	(42)	122	119	(18)	(51)	(24)
Depre-	IFM	—	—	—	(42)	—	—	—	(51)	—
ciation	50% Tax	139	131	(14)	(42)	137	127	(18)	(51)	(20)
	Dunkel	143	135	(14)	(43)	141	131	(18)	(52)	(20)
Net	FACTA	(131)	162	78	110	(145)	152	79	114	(0)
Operating	FSA	(232)	103	75	134	(245)	93	76	139	78
Income	IFM	—	—	—	16	—	—	—	20	—
	50% Tax	(268)	67	78	110	(282)	57	79	114	(0)
	Dunkel	(78)	215	115	135	(92)	205	117	139	(0)
Minus	FACTA	395	264	183	144	306	230	151	109	29
Off-Site	FSA	343	235	163	129	265	205	134	98	27
Costs	IFM	—	—	—	144	—	—	—	109	—
	50% Tax	395	264	183	144	306	230	151	109	29
	Dunkel	403	267	186	145	312	233	153	110	29
Net	FACTA	(526)	(102)	(106)	(34)	(450)	(78)	(72)	5	(30)
Economic	FSA	(575)	(132)	(88)	5	(510)	(112)	(58)	41	51
Value	IFM	—	—	—	(129)	—	—	—	(90)	—
	50% Tax	(526)	(102)	(106)	(34)	(450)	(78)	(72)	5	(30)
	Dunkel	(481)	(52)	(71)	(11)	(404)	(28)	(36)	29	(30)

— = not applicable.

CC = continuous conventional corn; CCBCB = conventional corn-soybean rotation; ACG = alternative cash grain; ACGF = alternative cash grain with fodder; ALLHAY = continuous alfalfa production. *See* Note 7.

Annex Table AV-5. Summary Results, Transition and Normal Periods, plus Present Value of Net Economic Value, Pennsylvania

Net Economic Value
($/ac/10 yr)

| | Policy | Conventional Tillage | | | | Reduced Tillage | | | | |
		CC	CCBCB	ACG	ACGF	CC	CCBCB	ACG	ACGF	ALLHAY
Gross	FACTA	202	753	522	462	172	727	515	453	95
Margin	FSA	(47)	607	486	508	(75)	581	480	501	247
	IFM	—	—	—	165	—	—	—	156	—
	50% Tax	(55)	576	522	462	(85)	550	515	453	95
	Dunkel	318	869	610	510	288	843	603	502	95
Minus	FACTA	259	244	(25)	(79)	255	237	(34)	(95)	(38)
Soil	FSA	231	230	(26)	(78)	228	222	(34)	(95)	(45)
Depre-	IFM	—	—	—	(79)	—	—	—	(95)	—
ciation	50% Tax	259	244	(25)	(79)	255	237	(34)	(95)	(38)
	Dunkel	267	252	(26)	(80)	263	245	(34)	(97)	(38)
Net	FACTA	(57)	509	547	541	(83)	490	549	548	133
Operating	FSA	(278)	377	512	587	(302)	359	514	596	292
Income	IFM	—	—	—	244	—	—	—	251	—
	50% Tax	(314)	332	547	541	(340)	313	549	548	133
	Dunkel	51	617	635	591	25	598	638	599	133
Minus	FACTA	738	492	342	269	570	429	281	204	55
Off-site	FSA	641	438	304	242	494	382	250	183	50
Costs	IFM	—	—	—	269	—	—	—	204	—
	50% Tax	738	492	342	269	570	429	281	204	55
	Dunkel	753	498	347	271	582	434	285	205	55
Net	FACTA	(795)	17	205	271	(654)	61	268	344	78
Value	FSA	(919)	(61)	208	345	(796)	(23)	264	413	243
	IFM	—	—	—	(26)	—	—	—	47	—
	50% Tax	(795)	17	205	271	(654)	61	268	344	78
	Dunkel	(702)	119	288	320	(556)	164	352	394	78

— = not applicable.

CC = continuous conventional corn; CCBCB = conventional corn-soybean rotation; ACG = alternative cash grain; ACGF = alternative cash grain with fodder; ALLHAY = continuous alfalfa production. *See* Note 7.

Annex Table AV-6. Summary Results, Net Economic Value, Nebraska

Net Economic Value
($/ac/4 yr)

	Policy	CC	HFCB	FOCB	ORGCB	HFROT	FOROT	ORGROT
					Rotation			
Gross	FACTA	166	531	534	503	345	343	331
Margin	FSA	119	501	503	473	351	348	334
	33% Tax	114	508	524	503	319	326	331
	IFM-Cong	—	—	—	—	362	359	346
	IFM-USDA	—	—	—	—	287	288	277
	Dunkel	198	570	572	539	376	373	359
Minus	FACTA	35	13	11	(9)	(6)	(5)	(13)
Soil	FSA	31	12	11	(8)	(5)	(4)	(12)
Depre-	33% Tax	35	13	11	(9)	(6)	(5)	(13)
ciation	IFM-Cong	35	13	11	(9)	(6)	(5)	(13)
	IFM-USDA	35	13	11	(9)	(6)	(5)	(13)
	Dunkel	36	13	12	(10)	(6)	(5)	(13)
Net	FACTA	132	519	523	513	351	348	344
Operating	FSA	88	489	492	482	356	352	346
Income	33% Tax	79	495	512	513	324	331	344
	IFM-Cong	—	—	—	—	367	364	346
	IFM-USDA	—	—	—	—	293	293	289
	Dunkel	162	557	560	549	382	378	373
Minus	FACTA	18	10	10	9	9	9	6
Off-Site	FSA	16	9	9	8	8	8	6
Costs	33% Tax	18	10	10	9	9	9	6
	IFM-Cong	—	—	—	—	9	9	6
	IFM-USDA	—	—	—	—	9	9	6
	Dunkel	18	10	10	9	9	9	6
Net	FACTA	114	509	512	504	342	339	337
Economic	FSA	72	480	483	474	348	344	340
Value	33% Tax	114	509	512	504	342	339	337
	IFM-Cong	—	—	—	—	358	355	353
	IFM-USDA	—	—	—	—	284	284	283
	Dunkel	144	547	549	540	373	369	366

— = not applicable.

CC = conventional continuous corn; HFCB = conventional corn-beans, w/herbicides and fertilizer; FOCB = corn-beans w/fertilizer but no herbicides; ORGCB = organic corn-beans; HFROT = corn-beans-corn-oats/clover with herbicides and fertilizer; FOROT = corn-bean-corn-oats/clover with fertilizer but no herbicides; ORGROT = organic corn-beans-corn-oats/clover.
See Note 7.

About the Authors

Miguel A. Altieri is an Associate Professor at the Division of Biological Control, University of California, Berkeley. He is the general coordinator of Sustainable Agriculture Networking and Extension (SANE), a UNDP-sponsored program. He also coordinates the research of Consorcio Latino Americano sobre Agroecologia y Desarollo (CLADES) in Latin America.

Carlos Benito is a Professor of Economics at the School of Business and Economics, Sonoma State University, California.

Paul Faeth is a Senior Associate in the Economics and Population Program at the World Resources Institute. He directs WRI's research on the economics of sustainable agriculture.

Andres Gomez-Lobo is an economist associated with Corporacion de Investigaciones Economicas para LatinoAmerica (CIEPLAN) in Chile, now on graduate study leave studying environmental economics in London.

R.P.S. Malik is an Associate Fellow at the Agricultural Research Centre, University of Delhi, India. He has completed numerous studies on various aspects of agricultural and resource economics including fertilizer use, irrigation, rural employment and farm energy use.

Prabhu Pingali is an Agricultural Economist and Leader of the Irrigated Rice Ecosystem Program at the International Rice Research Institute, Los Baños, Laguna, Philippines. He is actively involved in research on the environmental consequences of modern rice technology and was the leader of the multidisciplinary project that quantified the environmental and health effects of pesticide use in rice.

Agnes C. Rola is an Assistant Professor of Agricultural Economics at the University of the Philippines at Los Baños, College, Laguna, Philippines and concurrently is the Program Leader of Social Science and Policy Research at the Philippine Rice Research Institute. She has conducted research and field implementation of integrated pest management and has advised Philippine agencies on pesticide regulation and policy.

Tonci Tomic is a research fellow and consultant for the United Nations Food and Agriculture Organization Latin America regional office specializing in economic development for the region.

Jorge Valenzuela is a public policy specialist now with the Human Resources Division of the World Bank, Latin America Bureau.

John Westra is a Research Analyst in the Economics and Population Program at WRI.

References

Abbott, I. and C.A. Parker. 1981. "Interactions between earthworms and their soil environment." *Soil Biology and Biochemistry*, Vol. 131:191–7.

Abrol, I.P. and J.C. Katyal. Managing Soil Fertility for Sustained Agriculture. *In* Singh, R.P. (ed) 1990, *Sustainable Agriculture: Issues, Perspectives and Prospects in Semi-Arid Zones*. Indian Society of Agronomy 2.

Aiken, J.D. 1990. "Agrichemicals, Ground Water Quality and the 1990 Farm Bill." University of Nebraska Cooperative Extension, June 15.

Alam, M. Z. 1961. "Insect Pests of Rice in East Pakistan and their Control." East Pakistan Department of Agriculture, Dacca.

Aldridge, W.N. and M.K. Johnson. 1971. Side effects of organophosphorous compounds: delayed neurotoxicity. *Bulletin of the World Health Organization*, 44:259–263.

Alt, K., C.T. Osborn and D. Colacicco. 1989. *Soil Erosion: What Effect on Agricultural Productivity?* Agriculture Information Bulletin Number 556. Washington, D.C.: Economic Research Service, U.S. Department of Agriculture.

Altieri, M. A. 1987. *Agroecology: the scientific basis of alternative agriculture*. Boulder: Westview Press.

Ambur, Owen D. 1988. "Targeting Farm Aid Toward Efficiency." *Forum for Applied Research and Public Policy*, Summer 1988: 41–48.

American Society of Agricultural Engineers. 1984. *Erosion and soil productivity: Proceedings of the National Symposium on Erosion and Soil Productivity*. December 10–11, 1984, New Orleans, La.

Anderson, Jock R. 1974. "Sparse Data, Estimational Reliability, and Risk Efficient Decisions." *American Journal of Agricultural Economics*. August: 564–572.

Anderson, Jock R., J.L. Dillon and Brian Hardaker. 1980. "Agricultural Decision Analysis." Iowa State University Press, Ames, Iowa.

Anon. 1990. *Panorama Economico de la Agricultura*. No. 73. P. Santiago: Universidad Católica de Chile.

Antle, J.M. 1988. "Pesticide Policy, Production Risk and Producer Welfare: An Econometric Approach to Applied Welfare Economics." Resources for the Future. Washington, D.C.

Antle, J.M. and W.J. Goodger. 1984. "Measuring Stochastic Technology: The Case of Tulare Milk Production." *American Journal of Agricultural Economics*. August: 342–350.

Antle, J. M. and P. L. Pingali. 1991. "Pesticides, Farmer Health and Productivity: A Philippine Case Study." Paper presented at the International Association of Agricultural Economists, Tokyo, Japan, 22–29, August 1991. Also Social Sciences Division Paper No. 91-10.

Antle, John M. 1983a. "Incorporating Risk in Production Analysis." *American Journal of Agricultural Economics*. December: 1009–1106.

____. 1983b. "Sequential Decision Making." *American Journal of Agricultural Economics*. May: 281–290.

Aravena, R. 1988. "Degradación de insecticidas y acaricidas en manzanos de exportación." Tesis de Titulo, Fac. Ciencias Agrarias y Forestales, Univ. Chile. Mimeo, 92p.

Archibald, Sandra O. 1988. Incorporating Externalities into Agricultural Productivity Analysis. *In* Susan Capalbo and John Antle, eds. *Agricultural Productivity: Measurement and Explanation*. Resources for the Future, Washington, D.C.

Asian Development Bank. 1987. "Handbook on the Use of Pesticides in the Asia Pacific Region." Manila, Philippines.

____. 1989. Strengthening Pesticide Regulations, Report of the Workshop and Symposium.

Baeumer, K. and W.A.P. Bakerman. 1973. "Zero Tillage." *Advances in Agronomy*, Vol. 25: 78–123.

Bainova, A. 1982. Dermal absorption of pesticides. *In:* Toxicology of Pesticides, Copenhagen, WHO Regional Office for Europe, pp. 41-53 (European Cooperation on Environmental Health Aspects of the Control of Chemicals, Interim document 9).

Bakerman, W.A.P. and de Wit, C.T. 1970. "Crop husbandry on naturally compacted soils." *Netherlands Journal of Agricultural Science*, Vol. 18: 225–9.

Barker, R., R.W. Herdt with Beth Rose. 1985. "The Rice Economy of Asia." Published by Resources for the Future, Inc. Washington, D.C. with the International Rice Research Institute, Los Baños, Laguna, Philippines.

Barr, B.A., C.S. Koehler, and R. F. Smith. 1981. Crop rice losses, field losses due to insects, diseases, weeds and other pests. University of

California/Agency for International Development Pest Management and related environment protection project. University of California, Berkeley.

Batie, Saudra S. 1983. *Soil Erosion: Crisis in America's Croplands?* Washington D.C.: The Conservation Foundation.

Becker, Geoffrey S. Jan. 29, 1988. *Farm Support Programs: Their Purpose and Evolution*. CRS Report for Congress. Report No. 88-160 ENR. Washington, D.C.: Congressional Research Service, Library of Congress.

Benito, C. A. 1989. Degradación y Sostenibilidad en la Sierra Dominicana. Working Paper E-89/3. Berkeley, CA: Berkeley Research Institute.

____. 1988. *The microeconomics of shifting agriculture*. Berkeley Research Institute. Working Paper E-88/2. Berkeley, CA.

____. 1976. "Peasants' response to modernization projects in minifundia economies." *American Journal of Agric. Economies*, Vol. 58: 143–151.

Beppler, D.C., M.D. Shaw, and L.D. Hoffman. 1981. *Petroleum Energy Requirements for Pennsylvania Corn Production Systems*. University Park, Pa.: Pennsylvania State University.

Berardi, G.M. 1987. "Agricultural Export and Farm Policies: Implications for Soil Loss in the U.S." In *Agricultural Soil Loss: Processes, Policies, and Prospects*, ed. J.M. Harlin and G.M. Berardi. Boulder, Co.: Westview Press.

Bhalla, G.S., G.K. Chadha, S.P. Kashyap and R.K. Sharma. 1990. *Agricultural growth and structural change in the Punjab economy: an input-output analysis*. Research Report 82. Washington, D.C.: International Food Policy Research Institute.

Bhatia, R.K. 1988. "Energy Alternatives for Irrigation Pumping: An Economic Analysis for Northern India." *In* R. Bhatia & Armand Pereira. eds. *Socio Economic Aspects of Renewable Energy Technologies*. New York, New York: Praeger.

Bhatia, R. and R.P.S. Malik. 1985. *Choice of Technology for Pumping Irrigation Water: A Comparative Study of Energy Alternatives*. New Delhi: Centre for Economic Growth.

Binswanger, H.P. 1979. "Risk and Uncertainty in Agricultural Development: An Overview." In *Risk, Uncertainty and Agricultural Development*. Roumasset, Boussard and Singh (eds) SEARCA/ADC.

Binswanger, Hans. 1980. "Attitude Towards Risk: Experimental Measurement in Rural India." *American Journal of Agricultural Economics*. Vol. 62, pp. 395–407.

Blandford, D. 1990. "The Costs of Agricultural Protection and the Difference Free Trade Would Make." In *Agricultural Protectionism in The Industrialized World*, ed. F.H. Sanderson. Washington, D.C.: Resources for the Future.

Blevins, R.L., D. Cook, S.H. Phillips and R.E. Phillips. 1971. "Influence of no tillage on soil moisture." *Agronomy Journal*, Vol. 63.

Bovard, James. 1989. *The Farm Fiasco*. San Francisco, CA: Institute for Contemporary Studies.

Braunwald, (ed). 1987. Harrison's Internal Medicine.

Brown, L. R. and E. C. Wolf. 1984. *Soil erosion: quiet crisis in the world economy*. Washington, D.C.: Worldwatch Institute.

Bull, D. 1982. "A Growing Problem: Pesticides and the Third World Poor." Oxford: OXFAM Public Affairs Unit.

Bureau of Agricultural Research, D.A. 1989. *Technotrends*, Manila, Philippines.

Cacek, T and L.L. Langner. 1986. "The economic implications of organic farming." In, *American Journal of Alternative Agriculture*, Vol. I, No. 1: 25–29.

Campbell, David C. 1985. "Estimating Sedimentation Costs of Water Supply Storage." In *The Off-Site Costs of Soil Erosion: Proceedings of a Symposium held in May 1985*. Washington D.C.: The Conservation Foundation.

Carlson, G. A. 1984. "Risk-Reducing Inputs Related to Agricultural Pests." *Proceedings on Economic Analysis of Risk Management Strategies for Agricultural Production Firms*, March 25–28, 1984, New Orleans, Louisiana. pages 164–175.

_____. 1980. "Economic Aspects of Crop Loss Information, Crop Loss Assessment." Proceedings of E.C. Stakman Commemorative Symposium. University of Minnesota, Minneapolis, Minnesota.

_____. 1979. "Risk Reducing Inputs Related to Agricultural Pests." Mimeo paper of Department of Economics and Business, North Carolina State University, Raleigh, N.C.

Carr, A.B., W.H. Meyers, T.T. Phipps, and G.E. Rossmiller. 1988. *Decoupling Farm Programs*. Washington, D.C.: National Center for Food and Agricultural Policy, Resources for the Future.

Castañeda, C.P. 1987. A study of occupational pesticide exposure among Filipino farmers in San Leonardo, Nueva Ecija. *In* P.S. Teng and K. L. Heong, eds. Proceedings of the Southeast Asia Pesticide Management and Integrated Pest Management Workshop, February 23–27, 1987, Pattaya, Thailand.

Castañeda, C.P., N.C. Maramba and A. Ordas. 1990. "A field worker exposure study to methyl parathion among selected rice farmers." Report submitted to the Fertilizer and Pesticide Authority (FPA) and International Development Research Center (IDRC), Manila, Philippines.

Casteñeda, C. P., and A. C. Rola. 1990. Regional Pesticide Review: Philippines. A Country Report. Presented during the International Development Research Centre (IDRC) Regional Pesticide Review Meeting, 24 March 1990, Genting Highlands, Malaysia.

Cavanagh, J.B. 1954. The toxic effects of tri-ortho-cresyl phosphate on the nervous system: an experimental study in hens. *J. Neurol. Neurosurg. Psychiatry* 17: 163–172.

Chelliah, S. and E. A. Heinrichs, 1980. "Factors Affecting Insecticide Induced Resurgence of the Brown Planthopper, *Nilaparvata lugens* on Rice." *Environmental Entomology* 9:773–777.

Clark, E. H., J. A. Haverkamp, and W. Chapman. 1985. *Eroding Soils: The Off-Farm Impacts.* Washington, D.C.: The Conservation Foundation.

Clark, Edwin H., II. 1985. "National Estimates of the Off-Site Damages of Erosion." In *The Off-Site Costs of Soil Erosion: Proceedings of a Symposium Held in May 1985*, ed. Thomas E. Waddell. Washington, D.C: The Conservation Foundation.

Clark, Edwin H., II, J.A. Havercamp, and W. Chapman. 1985. *Eroding Soils: The Off-Farm Impacts.* Washington, D.C.: The Conservation Foundation.

Clothier, R., B. Johnson, and E. Reiner. 1981. "Interaction of Some Trialky Phosphorothiarates with Acetylcholinesterase: Characterization of Inhibition, Aging, and Reactivation. *Biochemistry Biophysiology Acta*, 660:306–16.

Colacicco, Daniel, Tim Osborn and Klaus Alt. 1989. "Economic damage from soil erosion." *Journal of Soil and Water Conservation*, Vol. 44, no. 1: 35–39.

Conway, Gordon R. 1986. *Agroecosystems Analysis for Research and Development.* Bangkok: Winrock International Institute for Agricultural Development.

Cooke, G.W. 1974. *The control of soil fertility.* London: English Language Book Society.

Copplestone, J. F. 1985. "Pesticide Exposure and Health in Developing Countries." *In* G. J. Turnbull, D. M. Sanderson and J. L. Bonsall, eds. *Occupational Hazards of Pesticide Use.* London and Philadelphia: Taylor and Francis.

Corbett, J. R. 1974. *The Biochemical Mode of Action of Pesticides.* London: Academic Press.

Council for Agricultural Science and Technology. 1980a. *Social and Economic Impacts of Restricting Pesticide Use in Agriculture.* Report No. 84. Ames, Iowa: Council for Agricultural Science and Technology.

_____. 1980b. *Organic and Conventional Farming Compared.* Report No. 84. Ames, Iowa: Council for Agricultural Science and Technology.

Coye, M. J., J. A. Lowe, and K. T. Moody. 1986. "Biological Monitoring of Agricultural Workers Exposed to Pesticides: I. Cholinesterase Activity Determinations." *Journal of Occupational Medicine* 28(8):619–27.

Cramer, H. H. 1967. "Plant Protection and World Crop Production." *Pflanzenschutz. Nachrichten Bayer.* 20:1–524.

Crosson, P. R. and A. T. Stout. 1983. *Productivity effects of cropland erosion in the United States.* Washington, D. C.: Resources for the Future.

Crosson, Pierre. 1986. "Soil Erosion and Policy Issues. *In* Phipps, Tim T., Pierre R. Crosson, and Kent A. Price. eds. *Agriculture and the Environment: The National Centre for Food and Agricultural Policy Annual Policy Review, 1986.* Washington, D.C.: Resources for the Future.

_____. 1985. "National Costs of Erosion on Productivity." *In Erosion Soil Productivity: Proceedings of the National Symposium on Erosion and Soil Productivity*, pp. 254–265, St. Joseph, Michigan: American Society of Agricultural Engineers.

_____. 1981. *Conservation Tillage and Conventional Tillage: A Comparative Assessment.* Ankeny, Iowa: Soil Conservation Society of America.

Crosson, Pierre, et. al. 1985. "A Framework for Analyzing the Productivity Costs of Soil Erosion in the U.S." *In* Follett and Stewart eds. *Soil Erosion and Crop Productivity*, pp. 482–502, Madison, Wisconsin: American Society of Agronomy.

Crosson, Pierre R. 1983. *Productivity Effects of Cropland Erosion in the United States.* Baltimore, Md.: Johns Hopkins University Press for Resources for the Future.

Crowder, B.M., et. al. 1984. *The Effects on Farm Income on Constraining Soil and Plant Nutrient Losses: An Application of the CREAMS Simulation Model.* Research Bulletin 850. University Park, Pa.: Agricultural Experiment Station, Pennsylvania, Penn State University.

Crutchfied, S. 1988. "Controlling Farm Pollution of Coastal Waters." In *Agricultural Outlook*, May issue. Washington, D.C.: Economic Research Service, USDA.

Culik, M.N., J.C. McAllister, M. C. Palada, and S.L. Rieger. 1983. *The Kutztown Farm Report: A Study of a Low-input Crop/Livestock Farm.* Technical Bulletin. Kutztown, Pa.: Regenerative Agriculture Library, Rodale Research Center.

Dabbert, S. and P. Madden. 1986. "The Transition to Organic Agriculture: A Multi-year model of a Pennsylvania Farm." *American Journal of Alternative Agriculture*, Vol. 1, No. 3: 99–107.

Daberkow, S. and M. Gill. 1989. "Common Crop Rotations Among Major Field Crops." In, *Agricultural Resources: Inputs Situation and Outlook Report.* Report No. AR-15. Washington, DC: Economic Research Service, U.S. Department of Agriculture.

Daberkow, S.G. and K.H. Reichelderfer. 1988. "Low-Input Agriculture: Trends, Goals, and Prospects of Input Use." *American Journal of Agricultural Economics*, Vol. 70, No. 5: 1159–1166.

Daffus, J. H. 1980. *Environmental Toxicology.* London: Edward Arnold Publishers, Ltd.

Daly, H.E. and J.B. Cobb, Jr. 1989. *For the Common Good: Redirecting the Economy toward Community, the Environment, and a Sustainable Future.* Boston: Beacon Press.

Davies, D.B. and R.Q. Cannell. 1975. "Review of experiments on reduced cultivation and direct drilling in the United Kingdom 1957–74." *Outlook on Agriculture*, Vol. 8: 216–20.

Davies, J. E.; V. H. Freed, and F. W. Whitemore. 1982. *An Agro-Medical Approach to Pesticide Management—Some Health and Environmental Considerations.* Miami: University of Florida, School of Medicine.

Day, Richard H. 1979. "Directions for Research on Economic Uncertainty." *In* Roumasset, Boussard, and Singh (eds.), *Risk, Uncertainty and Agricultural Development.*

De Janvry, Alain. 1972. "Optimal Levels of Fertilization Under Risk: The Potential for Corn and Wheat Fertilization Under Alternative Price Policies in Argentina." *American Journal of Agricultural Economics* 54(1):1–10.

Devadoss, S., et. al. 1989. *The FAPRI Modeling System at CARD: A Documentation Summary.* Technical Report 89-TR 13. Ames, Iowa: Center for Agricultural and Rural Development, Iowa State University.

Dewees, D. N.; C. K. Everson, and W. A. Sims. 1975. *Economic Analysis of Environmental Policies.* Toronto: University of Toronto Press for Ontario Economic Council.

Dhawan B.D. 1989. "Water Resources Management in India: Issues and Dimensions." *Indian Journal of Agricultural Economics*, Vol. 44, no. 3: 233–41.

Dobbs, T.L., M.G. Leddy and J.D. Smolik. 1988. "Factors influencing the economic potential for alternative farming systems: Case analyses in South Dakota." In, *American Journal of Alternative Agriculture*, Vol. 3, No. 1: 26–34.

Domanico, J.L., P. Madden, and E.J. Partenheimer. 1986. "Income effects of limiting soil erosion under organic, conventional and no-till systems in eastern Pennsylvania." *American Journal of Alternative Agriculture*, Vol. 1, No. 2: 75–82.

Dover, M. J. 1985. *A Better Mousetrap: Improving Pest Management for Agriculture*. Washington, D.C.: World Resources Institute.

Dum, S.A., F.A. Hughes, J.G. Cooper, B.W. Kelly and V.E. Crowley. 1981. *Farm Management Handbook*. University Park, Pennsylvania: College of Agriculture, Pennsylvania State University.

Dyke, P.T. and E.O. Heady. 1985. "Assessment of Soil Erosion and Crop Productivity with Economic Models." In *Soil Erosion and Crop Productivity*, ed. Follett and Stewart, pp. 105–117, Madison, Wisconsin: American Society of Agronomy.

Echeñique, J. L. and N. N. Rolando. 1989. *La Pequeña agricultura Agraria*. Santiago, Chile.

Ervin, C. A. and D. E. Ervin. 1982. "Factors affecting the use of soil conservation practices: hypotheses, evidence and policy implications." *Land Economics*, Vol. 58: 277–292.

Faeth, P., R. Repetto, K. Kroll, Q. Dai and G. Helmers. 1991. *Paying the Farm Bill: U.S. agricultural policy and the transition to sustainable agriculture*. Washington, D. C.: World Resources Institute.

FAI. 1989 and 1990. *Fertiliser Statistics: 1989*. New Delhi: Fertiliser Association of India.

Fajardo, F. F.; B. L. Canapi; G. V. Roldan; R. P. Escander; K. Moody; J. A. Litsinger; and T. W. Min. 1986. "A Survey on Farmers' Pest Management Practices on Rice in Guimba. Paper presented at the Pest Control Council of the Philippines Annual Conference, 8–10 May 1986, Iloilo City.

Fertilizer and Pesticides Authority. 1988. *FPA Pesticide Regulatory Policies and Implementing Guidelines and Procedures*. Manila.

Follett, R. F. and B. A. Stewart. 1985. *Soil Erosion and Crop Productivity*. Madison, Wisconsin: American Society of Agronomy.

Food and Agriculture Organization (FAO). 1989. *El impacto de la estrategias de desarrollo sobre los pobres rurales*. Rome: CMRADR.

Food and Agricultural Policy Research Institute (FAPRI). April, 1992. *Implications of a GATT Agreement for World Commodity Markets, 1993–98: An Analysis of the Dunkel Text on Agriculture*. FAPRI Staff Report #3-92. Ames, Iowa: Center for Agricultural and Rural Development, Iowa State University, in cooperation with Center for National Food and Agricultural Policy, University of Missouri-Columbia.

____. May, 1992. *1992 U.S. Agricultural Outlook*. Staff Report #1-92. Ames, Iowa: Center for Agricultural and Rural Development, Iowa State University.

____. 1990a. *Draft Report: An Evaluation of Price Support Equilibration Options for the 1990 Farm Bill*. Ames, Iowa: Center for Agricultural and Rural Development.

____. 1990b. *FAPRI U.S. Agricultural Outlook*. 1990 Spring Agribusiness Outlook and Policy Conference. Des Moines, Iowa. FAPRI.

____. 1988. *Policy Scenarios with the FAPRI Commodity Models*. Working Paper 88-WP 41. Ames, Iowa: Center for Agricultural and Rural Development, Iowa State University.

Fraser, D.G., J.W. Doran, W.W. Sahs, and G.W. Lesoing. "Soil Microbial Populations and Activities Under Conventional and Organic Management." *Journal of Environmental Quality*, Vol. 17 (1988): 585–590.

Frye, Wilbur W. 1987. "The Effects of Soil Erosion on Crop Productivity." In *Agricultural Soil Loss: Processes, Policies, and Prospects*, ed. J.M. Harlin and G.M. Berardi. Boulder, Co.: Westview Press.

Garcia, Lolita L. 1989. "Imperfect Information, Subjective Probability Estimates and Adoption of New Upland Rice Technology: *Claveria, Misamis Oriental*." M.S. thesis, University of the

Philippines at Los Baños. College, Laguna, Philippines.

Gardner, B.L. 1987. *The Economics of Agricultural Policies.* New York: Macmillan.

Gasto, J. C. 1982. "La agricultura." In, *Educación ambiental: hacia el desarrollo de una conducta ecologica en Chile*, ed. J. A. Martinez. Santiago: Univ. Metropolitana de Ciencias de la Educación.

Glass, E. H. 1976. "Pest Management: Principles and Philisophy." *In* J. Lawrence Apple and R. F. Smith (eds.) *Integrated Pest Management.* New York, N.Y.: Plenum Press.

Glass, E. H., and H. D. Thurston. 1978. "Traditional and Modern Crop Protection in Perspective." *Bioscience* 28(2):109–15.

Glass, E. H.; R. J. Smith, Jr.; I. J. Thomson, and H. D. Thurston. 1972. "Plant Protection Problems in Southeast Asia." Study conducted by Cornell University with support of U.S. Department of Agriculture, Agricultural Research Services.

Goldstein, W.A. and D.C. Young. 1987. "An Agronomic and Economic Comparison of a Conventional and a Low-input Cropping System in the Palouse." *American Journal of Alternative Agriculture*, Vol. 2, No. 2: 51–56.

Gomez, K. A.; R. W. Herdt; R. Barker, and S. K. de Datta. 1979. "A Methodology for Identifying Constraints to High Rice Yields on Farmers' Fields." In IRRI, *Farm-Level Constraints to High Rice Yields in Asia: 1974–77.*

Gomez, S. and J. Echeñique. 1988. *La agricultura chilena.* FLASCO-Agraria. Santiago.

Gonzalez, R. H. 1989. *Insectos y acaros de importancia agricola y cuarentenaria en Chile.* Santiago: BASF–Universidad de Chile.

_____. 1975. "Integrated pest control in orchards in Chile and perspectives in South America." *C.R.5 Symp. Lutte Integree on Vergers.* OILB/5ROP.

Gonzalez, R. H. and S. Rojas. 1966. "Estudio analitico del control biologico de plagas agricolas en Chile." *Agricultura Tecnica*, Vol. 26:133–147.

Gonzalez, R. H., M. A. Guerrero, and L. Lamborot. 1990. *Evaluación de las residuos de pesticidas detectados en los Estados Unidos en frutas y hortalizas chilenas.* Informative Agro-Economico No. 5. Santiago: Fundación Chile.

Goodell, G. E., Litsinger, J. A., and P.E. Kenmore. 1980. "Evaluating integrated pest management technology through interdisciplinary research at the farmer level." *In Future Trends of Integrated Pest Management*, pp. 72–75. International Organization for Biological Control (IOBC) Special Issue, London.

Goodell, Grace. 1984. "Challenges to International Pest Management Research and Extension in the Third World: Do We Really Want IPM to Work?" *Bulletin of the Entomological Society of America* 30(3):18–26.

Goudriaan, J. 1991. "Uncertainties in Biosphere/Atmosphere Exchanges, CO_2 Enhanced Growth." *Pure and Applied Chemistry*, Vol. 63, No. 5: 772–5.

Government of India. 1991. *Economic Survey 1990–91.* New Delhi: Government of India.

_____. 1990. *Annual Report on the Working of State Electricity Boards and Electricity Departments.* New Delhi: Planning Commission, Government of India.

_____. 1984. *A Guide For Estimating Irrigation Water Requirements.* Technical Series No. 2 (Revised), New Delhi: Ministry of Irrigation.

Government of Punjab 1989, 1990, 1991. *Statistical Abstract of Punjab.* Chandigarh: Government of Punjab, India.

_____. 1987. *Irrigation, Floods and Water Logging Statistics of Punjab (1986–87).* Chandigarh: Government of Punjab.

Governor's Soil Resources Study Commission. 1984. *Inland's Erosion and Sedimentation Situation*. Indianapolis, IN: Governor's Office.

GRC Economics. 1990. The value of crop protection chemicals and fertilizers to American agriculture and the consumer. Washington, D.C.: GRC Economics.

Grisley, W. and E.D. Kellog. 1983. "Farmers' Subjective Probability in Northern Thailand: An Elicitation Analysis." *American Journal of Ag. Economics* 65(1): pp. 74–82.

Hallberg, G.R. 1989. "Pesticide Pollution of Groundwater in the Humid United States." *Agriculture, Ecosystems and Environment*, Vol. 26: 299–367.

Hanson, James C., Dale M. Johnson, Steven E. Peters, and Rhonda R. Janke. 1990. *The Profitability of Sustainable Agriculture in the Mid-Atlantic Region: A Case Study Between 1981 and 1989*. Working Paper No. 90-12. College Park, Md.: Department of Agricultural and Resource Economics, University of Maryland.

Hardaker, J. B., and R. D. Ghodake. 1982. "Using Measurements of Risk Attitudes in Modelling Farmers' Technology Choices." International Crops Research Institute for the Semi-Arid Tropics Economic Program Progress Report. January 1982(60). Hyderabad, India.

Hardin, G. 1968. "The Tragedy of the Commons." *Science* 166:1103–07.

Harwood, J.L. and C.E. Young. 1989. *Wheat: Background for 1990 Farm Legislation*. AGES Staff Report No 89–56. Washington, D.C.: Economic Research Service, Commodity Economics Division, U.S. Department of Agriculture.

Harwood, R. R. 1988. "History of Sustainable Agriculture: An International Perspective." *Proceedings of the International Conference on Sustainable Agricultural Systems*. Columbus: Ohio State University.

Hayami, Y., and V. Ruttan. 1985. *Agricultural Development: An International Perspective*. Baltimore: Johns Hopkins University Press.

Hayes, W. J. 1982. *Pesticides Studied in Man*. Baltimore, Md.: Williams and Wilkins.

Headley, J. C. 1982. "The Economics of Pest Management." *In* R. S. Metcalf and W. H. Luckmann (eds.), *Introduction to Insect Pest Management*. New York, N.Y.: John Wiley and Sons.

____. 1972. "Defining the Economic Threshold." *In Pest Control Strategies for the Future*. Washington, D.C.: National Academy of Sciences.

Heady, E.O. 1948. "The Economics of Rotations with Farm and Production Policy Applications." *Journal of Farm Economics*, Vol. 30, No. 4: 645–664.

Heimlich, R.E. 1989. *Productivity and Erodibility of U.S. Cropland*. Agricultural Economic Report Number 604. Washington, D.C.: Economic Research Service, U.S. Department of Agriculture.

Heinrichs, E. A. 1988. "Role of Insect-Resistant Varieties in Rice IPM Systems." *In* P. S. Teng and K. L. Heong (eds.), *Pesticide Management and Integrated Pest Management in Southeast Asia*. Beltsville, Md.: International Crop Protection.

____. 1986. "Perspectives and Directions for the Continued Development of Insect-Resistant Rice Varieties." *Agriculture, Ecosystems and Environment*, 18:9–26.

Heinrichs, E. A.; G. B. Aquino; S. Chelliah; S. L. Valencia, and W. H. Reissig. 1982a. "Resurgence of *Nilaparvata lugens* (Stal) Populations as Influenced by Method and Timing of Insecticide Applications in Lowland Rice." *Environmental Entomology* 11(1):78–84.

Heinrichs, E. A., and O. Mochida. 1984. "From Secondary to Major Pest Status: The Case of Insecticide-Induced Rice Brown Planthopper, *Nilaparvata lugens*, Resurgence." *Protection Ecology* 7(2/3):201–18.

Heinrichs, E.A., H.R. Rapusas, G.B. Aquino and F. Palis. 1986. "Integration of Host Plant Resistance and Insecticides in the Control of Nepliotettix Virescens (Homoptera: Cicadellidae), a Vector of Rice Tungro Virus." *Journal of Economic Entomology*, Vol. 79, No. 2.

Heinrichs, E. A.; W. H. Reissig; S. L. Valencia, and S. Chelliah. 1982b. "Rates and Effect of Resurgence-Inducing Insecticides on Populations of *Nilaparvata lugens* (Homoptera: Delphacidae) and its Predators." *Environmental Entomology*, 11(6):1269–73.

Helmers, G.A., M.R. Langemeier, and J. Atwood. 1986. "An Economic Analysis of Alternative Cropping Systems for East-central Nebraska." *American Journal of Alternative Agriculture*, Vol. 1, No. 4: 153–158.

Heong, K. L. 1991. "Management of the Brown Planthopper in the Tropics." Paper presented at Symposium on Migration and Dispersal of Agricultural Insects, 25–28 September 1991, Tsukuba, Japan.

Herdt, R. W. 1987. A Retrospective View of Technological and Other Changes in Philippine Rice Farming 1965–82." *Economic Development and Cultural Change* 35(2):329–49.

_____. 1979. "An Overview of the Constraints Project Results." *In* IRRI, *Farm-Level Constraints to High Rice Yields in Asia: 1974–1977.*

Herdt, R. W., L. Castillo, and S. Jayasuriya. 1984. "The Economics of Insect Control in the Philippines." In IRRI, *Judicious and Efficient Use of Insecticides.*

Hicks, John R. 1946. *Value and Capital: An Inquiry into Some Fundamental Principles of Economic Theory.* Oxford: Oxford University Press.

Hock, W. K. 1987. "Pesticide Use: The Need for Proper Protection, Application and Disposal." In N. N. Ragsdale, and R.J. Kuhr (eds.), *Pesticides: Minimizing the Risks.* Developed from a symposium sponsored by the Division of Agrochemicals at the 191st meeting of the American Chemical Society, 13–18 April 1986, New York, N.Y. Washington, D.C.: American Chemical Society.

Hrubovcak, J., M. LeBlanc, and J. Miranowski. 1990. "Limitations in Evaluating Environmental and Agrichemical Policy Coordination Benefits." In, *AEA Papers and Proceedings: Environmental and Agricultural Policies*, Vol. 80, No. 2: 208–212.

Huelgas, Z. M. 1989. "Risk in Production, Pest Control and Productivity of Pesticides in Irrigated Lowland Rice, Philippines." M.S. thesis, University of the Philippines at Los Baños, Laguna, Philippines.

IICA. 1990. *Coeficientes técnicos de producción de los principales frutales del pais.* Santiago: IICA-Subsecretaria de Agricultura de Chile.

Instituto Nacional de Estadisticas. 1987. *Estadisticas agropecuarias.* Santiago: I.N.E.

International Rice Research Institute (IRRI). 1990. World Rice Statistics.

_____. 1988. "Insecticide Evaluation for 1986." Entomology Department, Los Baños, Laguna.

_____. 1977. "Constraints to High Yields on Asian Rice Farms: An Interim Report." Los Baños, Laguna.

IREN. 1979. *Fragilidad de los Ecosistemas Naturales de Chile.* Inform. #40. Santiago: Inst. Nac. de Inv. de Rec. Nat.-CORFO.

Ishii, S., and C. Hirano. 1959. "Effect of Fertilizers on the Growth of the Larvae of the Rice Stemborer, Chilo suppressalis Walker." *In* Growth Response of the Larva to Rice Stem Plant Cultured in Different Nitrogen Level Soils. *Japanese Journal of Applied Entomology and Zoology* 2(3):198–202.

Ishikura, H. 1984. "Projected Trend in the Use of Insecticides in Rice Insect Pest Control." In

Indicious and Efficient Use of Insecticides on Rice. Manila: IRRI.

Jaeger, K. W. 1976. "Organophosphate Exposure from Industrial Usage, Electroneuromyography in Occupational Medical Supervision of Exposed Workers." In *Pesticides-induced Delayed Neurotoxicity*. Proceedings of a Conference, 19–20 February 1976, Washington, D.C.: U.S. Environmental Protection Agency. (Environmental Health Effects Research Series: EPA-600/1-76-025).

Jain, K.K., H.S. Bal, and I.P. Singh. 1989. "Economic Analysis of Irrigation in Punjab." *Indian Journal of Agricultural Economics*, Vol. 44, no. 3: 291.

Jarvis, L. S. 1985. *Chilean agriculture under military rule*. Berkeley: Institute of International Studies, University of California.

Jose, H.D., et. al. 1989. *Estimated Crop and Livestock Production Costs—1989*. Nebraska Cooperative Extension EC-872.

Jurenas, Remy. *U.S. Agricultural Import Protection and GATT Negotiations*. CRS Issue Brief. Washington, D.C.: Environment and Natural Resources Policy Division, Congressional Research Service, The Library of Congress.

Just, Richard E. and Rulon D. Pope. 1979. "Production Function Estimation and Related Risk Considerations." *American Journal of Agricultural Economics* 61(2):276–84.

_____. 1976. "Input Decisions and Risk." In Roumasset, Boussard, and Singh, *Risk, Uncertainty and Agricultural Development*.

Kahn, J.R. 1987. "Economic damage from herbicide pollution in Chesapeake Bay." *Project Appraisal*, Vol. 2, No. 3: 142–152.

Karvonen, M., and M. I. Mikheev. 1986. *Epidemiology of Occupational Health*. WHO Regional Publications, European Series No. 20. Copenhagen, Denmark.

Kenmore, P. E. 1987. "Crop Loss Assessment in a Practical Integrated Pest Control Program for Tropical Asian Rice." *In* P. S. Teng (ed.), *Crop Loss Assessment and Pest Management*. St. Paul, Minn.: American Phytopathological Society Press, pp. 225–41.

_____. 1980. "Ecology and Outbreaks of a Tropical Insect Pest of the Green Revolution: The Rice Brown Planthopper *Nilaparvata lugens* (Stal)." Ph.D. diss., University of California, Berkeley.

Kenmore, P. E.; F. O. Cariño; C. A. Perez; V. A. Dyck, and A. P. Gutierrez. 1984. "Population Regulation of the Rice Brown Planthopper (*Nilaparvata lugens* Stal) within Rice Fields in the Philippines," *Journal of Plant Protection in the Tropics* 1(1):19–37.

Kenmore, P. E.; J. A. Litsinger; J.P. Bandong; A. C. Santiago, and N. M. Salac. 1987. "Philippine Rice Farmers and Insecticides: Thirty Years of Growing Dependency and New Options for Change." *In* J. Tait and B. Napompeth (eds.), *Management of Pests and Pesticides: Farmers' Perception and Practices*. Boulder, Col.: Westview Press.

Kerrigan, G. R. 1984. Evaluacion del sistema de agricultura organica en los cultivos de frejol y maiz. Tesis Ing. Agr. Univ. de Chile. Santiago.

Kiritani, K. 1979. "Integrated Insect Pest Management for Rice in Japan." Paper presented at IRRI Research Conference, Los Baños, Philippines, 16–20 April 1979.

Knutson, Ronald D., C. Robert Taylor, John B. Penson, and Edward G. Smith. 1990. *Economic Impacts of Reduced Chemical Use*. College Station, Texas: Knutson & Associates.

Koenig, Steve & Jerome Stam. 1993. "Farm Finance." *Agricultural Outlook*, April: 23–25.

Krissoff, Barry, John Sullivan, John Wainio and Brian Johnston. 1990. *Agricultural Trade Liberalisation and Developing Countries*. ERS Staff Report No. AGES 9042. Agriculture and

Trade Analysis Division, Economic Research Service, US Department of Agriculture.

Kulkarni, B.K. and N.K. Sawant. 1977. "Effect of soil compaction on root cation exchange capacity of crop plants." *Plant and Soil*, Vol. 48: 269–78.

Lal, R. 1981. "No-tillage farming in the tropics." In *No Tillage Research: Research Reports and Reviews*, R.E. Phillips et. al. ed. Lexington: University of Kentucky.

Lal R. and F.J. Pierce, 1991. The Vanishing Resource. *In* R. Lal and F.J. Pierce (eds), *Soil Management for Sustainability*. Soil and Water Conservation Society. Ankeny, Iowa.

Langley, James. March, 1992. *A Guide to Planting Flexibility*. Washington, D.C.: Agricultural Stabilization and Conservation Service, U.S. Department of Agriculture.

Larson, W. E., F. J. Pierce, and R. H. Dowdy. 1983. "The threat of soil erosion to long-term crop production." *Science*, Vol. 29:458–462.

Larson, W.E., et. al. 1985. "Effects of Soil Erosion on Soil Properties as Related to Crop Productivity and Classification." In *Soil Erosion and Crop Productivity*, ed. Follett and Stewart, pp. 190–210, Madison, Wisconsin: American Society of Agronomy.

Levin, H. S., and L. Rodnitzky. 1976. "Behavioral Effects of Organophosphate Pesticides in Man." *Clinical Toxicology* 9(3):391–405.

Lewis, H. W., M. F. Mertens, and J. A. Steen. 1973. "Behavioral Changes from Chronic Exposure to Pesticides Used in Aerial Application: Effects of Phosdrin on the Performance of Monkeys and Pigeons on Variable Interval Reinforcement Schedules." *Aerospace Medicine* 44(3):290–93.

Litsinger, J. A. 1990. "Integrated Pest Management in Rice: Impact on Pesticide." Workshop on Environmental and Health Impacts of Pesticide Use in Rice Culture, 28–30 March, 1990. Los Baños, Laguna, Philippines: International Rice Research Institute.

_____.1987. "Integrated Pest Management Assessment in Farm Communities." Paper presented at Workshop on Integrated Pest Management and Integrated Nutrient Management on Rice, 28–29 July 1987, IRRI.

_____. 1984. "Assessment of Need-Based Insecticide Application for Rice." Paper presented at MA–IRRI Technology Transfer Workshop.

Litsinger, J.A. et al. Rice Crop Loss from Insect Pests in Wetland and Dryland Environments of Asia with Emphasis on the Philippines. *Insect Sci. Application* 8:677–692.

Lockeretz, W., G. Shearer, D.H. Kohl, and R.W. Klepper. 1984. "Comparison of Organic and Conventional Farming in the Corn Belt." In, *Organic Farming: Current Technology and Its Role in a Sustainable Agriculture*. Madison, Wisconsin.

Loevinsohn, M. F. 1987. "Insecticide Use and Increased Mortality in Rural Central Luzon, Philippines." *Lancet* 1(8546):1359–62.

_____. 1985. "Agricultural Intensification and Rice Pest Ecology: Lessons and Implications." Paper presented at IRRI Conference, 1–5 June 1985, Los Baños, Philippines.

Loevinsohn, M. E.; J. A. Litsinger; J. P. Bandong; A. Alviola, and P. Kenmore. 1982. "Synchrony of Rice Cultivation and the Dynamics of Pest Population Experimentation and Implementation." Paper presented at the IRRI Saturday Seminar, August 28, 1982, Los Baños, Philippines.

Lotti, M. 1987. "Assessment of Human Exposure to Pesticides." *In* L. G. Costa; C. L. Galli, and S. D. Murphy (eds.), *Experimental, Clinical and Regulatory Perspectives*, vol. 13. Berlin/Heidelberg: Springer-Verlag/NATO Advanced Study Institute for Toxicology for Pesticides.

Lowrance, R., P.F. Hendrix, and E.P. Odum. 1986. "A hierarchical approach to sustainable agriculture." *American Journal of Alternative Agriculture*, Vol. 1, No. 4: 169–173.

Marciano, V. P.; A. Mandac, and J. C. Flinn. 1981. "Insect Management Practices of Rice Farmers in Laguna." *Philippine Journal of Crop Science* 6(1 and 2):14–20.

Marquez, C.B., P.L. Pingali and F.G. Palis, 1992. Farmer Health Impact of Long Term Pesticide Exposure - A Medical and Economic Analysis in the Philippines. IRRI.

Marquez, C.B. P.L. Pingali, F.G. Palis, V.C. Rodriguez and M.G.E. Ramos. 1991. "Evaluation of the Health Effects of Pesticide Use Among Laguna Farmers." International Rice Research Institute, Los Baños, Philippines.

Mech, S.J. and D.M. Smith. 1967. "Water erosion under irrigation." In *Irrigation of Agricultural Lands*, ed. R.M. Hagan, et. al. Madison, Wisconsin: American Society of Agronomy, 950–63.

Medina, J. R., and V. Justo. 1990. "Effect of Pesticide Use on Insect Populations in a Ricefield Agro-Ecosystem." Paper presented during the workshop on Environmental and Health Impact of Pesticide Use in Rice Culture, 28–30, March 1990. Laguna, Philippines: International Rice Research Institute.

Mercado, R. D. 1976. *Manual of Health Basic Statistics*. Manila: Institute of Public Health.

Mercier, S. 1989. *Corn: Background for 1990 Farm Legislation*. Staff Report No. AGES 89-47. Washington, D.C.: Economic Research Service, Commodity Economics Division, U.S. Department of Agriculture.

Metcalf, D. R., and J. H. Holmes. 1969. "EEG, Psychological and Neurological Alterations in Humans with Organophosphorous Exposure." *Annals of the New York Academy of Sciences* 16:357–65.

Metcalf, R. L. 1984. "Trends in the Use of Chemical Insecticides." *In Proceedings of FAO/IRRI Workshop on Judicious and Efficient Use of Insecticides on Rice.* Manila: IRRI, pp. 69–91.

Metcalf, R. L., and W. Luckman. 1975. "The Pest Management Concept." *In* R.L. Metcalf and W. Luckman (eds.), *Introduction to Insect Pest Management*. New York, N.Y.: John Wiley and Sons.

Mcyer, L.D., et. al. 1985. "Experimental Approaches for Quantifying the Effect of Soil Erosion on Productivity." In *Soil Erosion and Crop Productivity*, ed. Follett and Stewart, pp. 214–232, Madison, Wisconsin: American Society of Agronomy.

Ministerio de Agricultura. 1989. *El sector Agricola Chileno: politicas y resultados*. Santiago: Ministry of Agriculture.

Moody, K. 1982. "The Status of Weed Control in Rice in Asia." *FAO Plant Protection Bulletin* 30:119–23.

Morgan, D. P. 1977. "Recognition and Management of Pesticide Poisonings." 2d Ed. U.S. Environmental Protection Agency, Office of Pesticide Programs, Washington, D.C.

Moscardi, E., and A. de Janvrey. 1977. "Attitudes Toward Risk Among Peasants: An Econometric Approach." *American Journal of Agricultural Economics* 59(4):710–16.

Mumford, J. D. 1987. "Analysis of Decision-Making in Pest Management." Teng (ed), *Crop Loss Assessment and Pest Management*. The American Phytopathological Society, U.S.A.

___ 1982. "Perceptions and Losses from Pests of Arable Crops by Some Farmers in England and New Zealand." *Crop Protection* 1:283–288.

___ 1981. "Pest Control Decision-Making: Sugar Beet in England. *Journal of Agricultural Economics* 32: 31–41.

National Erosion-Soil Productivity Research

Committee. 1981. "Soil Erosion Effects on Soil Productivity." In Follett and Stewart ed. *Soil Erosion and Crop Productivity*. Madison, Wisconsin: American Society of Agronomy.

National Research Council. 1989. *Alternative Agriculture*. Washington, D.C.: National Academy Press.

Nielsen, E.G. and L.K. Lee. 1987. *The Magnitude and Costs of Groundwater Contamination From Agricultural Chemicals: A National Perspective*. Agricultural Economic Report Number 576. Washington, D.C.: Economic Research Service, U.S. Department of Agriculture.

Niswonger, C. Rollin and Philip E. Fess. 1977. *Accounting Principles (12th Edition)*. Cincinnati: South-Western Publishing Company.

Norton, G. A., and J. D. Mumford. 1983. "Decision-Making in Pest Control." In T. H. Cooker, (ed.), *Applied Biology*, vol. 8. New York, N.Y.: Academic Press.

O'Connell, P. 1990. Briefing Materials on Sustainable Agriculture Activities in USDA. Not published. Cooperative State Research Service, U.S. Department of Agriculture.

Occupational Health and Safety for Agricultural Workers: Agricultural Health & Safety Considerations for a Rural Primary Health Care System. Community Health Clinics, Inc., Nampa, Idaho, Dec. 1976.

Orland, M., and R. Saltman. 1981. *Manual of Medical Therapeutics*. Boston, Mass.: Little Brown and Co.

Orticio, H. M. 1975. "Increased Agricultural Production. Masagana Program Viewpoint of an Implementing Agency." In *Effective Delivery of Extension Services and the Masagana Program*. Los Baños, Laguna, Philippines: Center for Policy and Development Studies.

Otsuka, Keijiro, and Fe Gascon. 1990. "Two Decades of Green Revolution in Central Luzon: A Study of Technology Adoption and Productivity Changes." *IRRI Social Science Division Paper* No. 90-15, Los Baños.

Oudejans, J. A. 1982. "Agro-Pesticides: Their Management and Application." Bangkok: Economic and Social Commission for Asia and the Pacific.

Palis, F. G.; P. L. Pingali, and J. A. Litsinger. 1990. "A Multiple-Pest Economic Threshold for Rice (A Case Study in the Philippines)." In Teng (ed). *Crop Loss Assessment in Rice*. [IRRI].

Pathak, M. D., and V. A. Dyck. 1973. "Developing an Integrated Method of Rice Insect Pest Control." *Pest Articles and News Summary* 19(4):534–44.

Pathak, P. K., and G. S. Dhaliwal. 1981. "Trends and Strategies for Rice Pest Problems in Tropical Asia." IRRI Research Paper Series 64, Los Baños.

Penn State Agricultural Extension Service. 1987. *Penn State Agronomy Guide*. University Park, Pa.: Pennsylvania State University.

Phillips, R.E., R.L. Blevins, G.W. Thomas, W.W. Frye and S.H. Phillips. 1980. "No-Tillage Agriculture." *Science*, Vol. 208.

Phipps, T.T. and K. Reichelderfer. 1989. "Farm support and environmental quality at odds?" *Resources*, Spring: 14–15.

_____. 1988. *Agricultural Policy and Environmental Quality*. Washington, D.C.: Resources for the Future.

Pierce, F.J., W.E. Larson, R.H. Dowdy, and W. Graham. 1983. "Productivity of Soils: Assessing long-term change due to erosion." *Journal of Soil and Water Conservation*, Vol. 38: 39–44.

Pimentel, D., G. Berardi and S. Fast. 1983. "Energy efficiency of farming systems: organic and conventional agriculture." *Agric. Ecosyst. and Environm.*, Vol. 9:359–372.

Pimentel, D. and L. Levitan. 1986. "Pesticides: amounts applied and amounts reaching pests." *Bio Science*, Vol. 36:86–90.

Pimentel, David. 1987. "Soil Erosion Effects on Farm Income." In J.M. Harlin and G.M. Berardi, eds. *Agricultural Soil Loss: Processes, Policies, and Prospects,* Boulder, Co.: Westview Press.

Pimentel, David, et. al. 1980. "Environmental and social costs of pesticides: a preliminary assessment." *Oikos*, Vol. 34:126–140.

Pingali, P. L., and G. A. Carlson. 1985. "Human Capital, Adjustments in Subjective Probabilities, and the Demand for Pest Control." *American Journal of Agricultural Economics* 67(4):853–61.

Pingali, P. L., and C. B. Marquez. 1990. "Health Costs of Long-Term Pesticide Exposure in the Philippines—A Medical and Economic Analysis." *IRRI Social Science Division Paper* No. 90-04, Los Baños, Laguna, Philippines.

Pingali, P. L., C. B. Marquez, and Florencia G. Palis. 1992. "Farmer Health Impact of Long Term Pesticide Exposure—A Medical and Economic Analysis for the Philippines." Paper presented at a workshop on "Measuring the Health and Environmental Effects of Pesticides," 30 March–3 April 1992, Bellagio, Italy.

Pingali, P. L.; P. F. Moya, and L. E. Velasco. 1990. "The Post-Green Revolution Blues in Asian Rice Production—The Diminished Gap Between Experiment Station and Farmer Yields. *IRRI Social Science Division Paper* No. 90-01, Los Baños, Laguna, Philippines.

Pingali, P. L.; F. G. Palis, and V. Rodriguez. 1989. "Pesticide Externalities in Asian Rice Production: Progress Report." Paper presented at the Progress Reports Meeting of the Environmental Costs of Chemical Input Use in Southeast Asian Rice Production, 31 October. Los Baños, Laguna, Philippines: International Rice Research Institute.

Poincelot, Raymond P. 1986. *Toward a More Sustainable Agriculture*. Westport, CT: AVI Publishing Co., Inc.

Prihar, S.S. and S.S. Grewal. 1988. "Improving Irrigation Water Use Efficiency in Rice-Wheat Cropping Sequence: Technical and Policy Issues." In *Seminar on Water Management: The Key to Developing Agriculture,* ed. J.S. Kanwar. New Delhi: Agricole Publishing Academy.

Punjab Agricultural University. 1990. *Package of Practices for Rabi (1989–90) and Kharif (1990).* Ludhiana: Punjab Agricultural University.

____. 1990. *Punjab Agricultural Handbook*. Ludhiana: Punjab Agricultural University.

____. 1989. *Twenty Seventh Annual Report*. Ludhiana: Department of Soils, Punjab Agricultural University.

____. 1987. *ICAR Coordinated Project for Research on Water Management, Annual Progress Report 1986–87*. Ludhiana: Punjab Agricultural University.

____. 1986. *Twenty Fourth Annual Report*. Ludhiana: Department of Soils, Punjab Agricultural University.

Ragsdake and R.J. Kuhr (eds). 1987. Pesticide Use: The need for proper protection, application and disposal. *In* Pesticides (Minimizing the Risks), Pennsylvania, U.S.A.

Rawson, Jean M. 1992. Agricultural Issues in the 102d Congress. CRS Issue Brief. Washington, D.C.: Environment and Natural Resources Policy Division, Congressional Research Service, Library of Congress.

Reichelderfer, K. H. n.d. "Economic Opportunities and Constraints in the Development of Pest Management Systems with Low Input Technology." Paper presented for U.S. Department of Agriculture, Economic Research Service, at 11th International Congress on Plant Protection, 5–9 October 1987, Manila. Processed.

Reid, I. 1979. "Seasonal changes in microtopography and surface depression storage in soils. In *Man's impact on the hydrological cycle in the United Kingdom*, ed. G.E. Hollis. Norwich: Geo Abstracts, 19–30.

Reid, W.S. 1985. "Regional Effects of Soil Erosion on Crop Productivity." *In* Follett and Stewart eds. *Soil Erosion and Crop Productivity*, pp. 235–249, Madison, Wisconsin: American Society of Agronomy.

Reissig, W. H., E. A. Heinrichs, and S. L. Valencia. 1982a. "Insecticide Induced Resurgence of the Brown Planthopper, *Nilaparvata lugens*, on Rice Varieties with Different Levels of Resistance." *Environmental Entomology* 11(1):165–68.

_____. 1982b. "Effects of Insecticides on *Nilaparvata lugens* and Its Predators: Spiders, *Microbelia atrolineata* and *Cyrtorhinus lividipennis*." *Environmental Entomology* 11(1):193–99.

Repetto, R., W. Magrath, M. Wells, C. Beer, and F. Rossini. 1989. *Wasting Assets: Natural Resources in the National Income Accounts*. Washington, D.C.: World Resources Institute.

Ribaudo, Marc. Personal interview. July 10, 1990. U.S. Department of Agriculture, Economic Research Service, Washington, D.C.

Ribaudo, Marc O. 1989. *Water Quality Benefits from the Conservation Reserve Program*. Agricultural Economic Report No. 606. February 1989. Resources and Technology Division, Economic Research Service. U.S. Department of Agriculture.

_____. 1985. "Regional Estimates of Off-Site Damages From Soil Erosion." In *The Off-Site Cost of Soil Erosion, Proceedings of a Symposium Held in May 1985*, ed. Thomas E. Waddell. Washington, D.C.: The Conservation Foundation.

Roberts, D. V. 1980. *Blood Cholinesterase Monitoring of Workers Exposed to Organophosphorous Pesticides: Theory and Practice in Field Worker Exposure During Pesticide Application*. New York, N.Y.: Elsevier Scientific Publishing Company.

Rodas, A. and F. Chanduvi. 1989. *Problematica de la degradacion de suelos y aguas por salinizacion en el valle de Copiapo Chile*. 87p. Santiago, Chile: Food and Agricultural Organization.

Roger, P. A., K. L. Heong, and P. S. Teng. 1991. "Biodiversity and Sustainability of Wetland Rice Production: Role and Potential of Microorganisms and Invertebrates." *In* D. L. Hawksworth (ed.), *The Biodiversity of Microorganisms and Invertebrates: Its Role in Sustainable Agriculture*. Wallingford, Heartsfordshire, U.K.: CAB International, pp. 117–36.

Roger, P. A., and Y. Kurihara. 1988. "Floodwater Biology of Tropical Wetland Ricefields." In *Proceedings of the First International Symposium on Paddy Soil Fertility*, 6–13 December 1988, University of Chiang Mai, Chiang Mai, Thailand. IRRI Published Papers, 1988 No. 32, Los Baños.

Rola, A. C. 1989. "Pesticides, Health Risks and Farm Productivity: A Philippine Experience." Agricultural Policy Reseach Program Monograph No. 89-01, University of the Philippines at Los Baños.

Rola, A. C., A. R. Chupungco, C. B. Adalla, M. M. Hoque, T. H. Stuart, and B. R. Sumayao. 1988. "Results of the Benchmark Survey." Integrated Pest Management Extension and Women Project. College, Laguna, Philippines.

Rola, A. C., A. R. Chupungco, R. A. Corcolon, and J. T. Hernandez. 1992. "Pesticide and Pest Management in the Philippines: A Policy Perspective." Draft Report for International Development Research Center. University of the Philippines at Los Baños, Laguna, Philippines.

Rola, A.C., E. E. Dumayas, P. A. Alcaide, E. C. Catolin, R. A. Corcolon, and J. T. Hernandez. 1990. "The Socioeconomics of IPM in Lowland Rice–Based Farming Systems." Terminal Report submitted to International Development

Research Center. University of the Philippines at Los Baños, Laguna, Philippines.

Rook, Sarah P., and G. A. Carlson. 1985. "Participation in Pest Management Groups." *American Journal of Agricultural Economics* 67(3):563–66.

Rosegrant, M. W., and P. L. Pingali. 1991. "Sustaining Rice Productivity Growth in Asia: A Policy Perspective." IRRI Social Science Division Papers, No. 91–01.

Roumasset, J. A., J. M. Boussard, and I. Singh. 1979. *Risk, Uncertainty and Agricultural Development*. Laguna, Philippines: Southeast Asian Regional Center for Graduate Study and Research on Agriculture/Agricultural Development Council.

Runge, C. Ford. 1986. "Induced Innovation in Agriculture and Environmental Quality." *In* Phipps, Crosson, and Price eds. *Agriculture and the Environment*. Washington, D.C.: Resources for the Future.

Runge, C.F., R.D. Munson, E. Lotterman and J. Creason. 1990. *Agricultural Competitiveness, Farm Fertilizer and Chemical Use, and Environmental Quality: A Descriptive Analysis*. St. Paul, Minnesota: Center for International Food and Agricultural Policy, University of Minnesota.

Russell, E.W. 1977. "The role of organic matter in soil fertility." *Philosophical Transactions of the Royal Society of London*, B 281. London: Royal Society of London.

Sahs, W.W. and G. Lesoing. 1990. Progress Report, University of Nebraska Agricultural Research Project 12–58, Jan. 25, 1990.

_____. 1985. "Crop Rotations and Manure Versus Agricultural Chemicals in Dryland Grain Production." *Journal of Soil and Water Conservation*, Vol. 40: 511–516.

Scandizzo, P. L., and J. L. Dillon. 1979. "Peasant Agriculture and Risk Preferences in Northeast Brazil: A Statistical Sampling Approach." *In*

Roumasset, Boussard, and Singh (eds.), *Risk, Uncertainty and Agricultural Development*.

Schaffer, J.D. and G.W. Whittaker. "Average Farm Incomes: They're Highest Among Farmers Receiving the Largest Direct Government Payments." *Choices*, Second Quarter, 1990, 30–31.

Scherer, D., and T. Attig (eds.). 1983. *Ethics and the Environment*. Englewood Cliffs, N.J.: Prentice-Hall.

Schertz, D.L., W.C. Moldenhauer, S.J. Livingston, G.A. Weesies, and E.A. Hintz. "Effect of past soil erosion on crop productivity in Indiana." In, *Journal of Soil and Water Conservation*, November–December 1989: 604–608.

Schlesselman, J. J., and P. D. Stolley. 1982. *Case-Control Studies: Design, Conduct, Analysis*. New York, N.Y., and Oxford, U.K.: Oxford University Press.

Sepulveda, E., J. Sepulveda and P. del Real. 1990. *Manejo integrado de plagas desde la perspectiva de las Organizaciones Sindicales Campesinas Chilenas*. Santiago: Comision Nacional Campesina-AGRA.

Shepard, B. Merle, and Abdul Latif Isa. 1987. "Integrated Pest Management in Rice: Philippines and Egypt." Paper presented at the International Symposium on Rice Farming Systems: New Directions, 31 January–3 February, Agricultural Research Center (Cairo University Street), Giza, Egypt.

Shrader, W.O. and R.D. Voss. 1980. "Soil Fertility: Crop Rotation vs. Monoculture." *Crop and Soil Magazine*, Vol. 7: 15–18.

Sillers, Donald Arthur, III. 1980. "Measuring Risk Preferences of Rice Farmers in Nueva Ecija, Philippines: An Experimental Approach." Ph.D. diss., Yale University, New Haven, Conn.

Singh. B. 1975. "Are Fertilisers Polluting Groundwater?" *Everyday Science*, Vol. 20, no. 2.

Singh, B. and H.S. Bal. 1987. "Indiscriminate Fertiliser Use Vis-a-Vis Groundwater Pollution in Central Punjab." *Indian Journal of Agricultural Economics*, Vol. 42, no. 3: 404–9.

Singh, B. and G.S. Sekhon. 1976. "Nitrate Pollution of Groundwater from Nitrogen Fertiliser and Animal Wastes in the Punjab, India." *Agriculture and Environment*, Vol. 3: 57–67.

Singh, Gurcharan. 1987. "Correlation of Unit Draft of Electric Tubewells and Irrigation Requirements of Crops in Selected Areas of Punjab—A Case Study." *Proceedings of National Symposium on Hydrology*, Roorkee, India.

Smith, J.; J. A. Litsinger; J. P. Bandong; M.D. Lumaban, and C. G. de la Cruz. 1989. "Economic Thresholds for Insecticide Application to Rice: Profitability and Risk Analysis to Filipino Farmers." *Journal of Plant Protection in the Tropics* 6(1):61–87.

Smith, K. R., R. A. Carpenter, and M. S. Faulstich. 1988. "Risk Assessment of Hazardous Chemical Systems in Developing Countries." East-West Environment and Policy Institute, Occasional Paper #5, Honolulu, Hawaii.

Smith, R.A., R.B. Alexander, and M.G. Wolman. 1987. "Water-Quality Trends in the Nation's Rivers." *Science*, Vol. 235: 1607–1615.

Smith, R. F. 1972. "The Impact of the Green Revolution on Plant Protection in Tropical and Subtropical Areas." *Bulletin of the Entomological Society of America* 18(1): 7–14.

Smith, R. F., J. L. Apple, and D. Bottrell. 1976. "The Origins of IPM Concepts for Agricultural Crops." J. L. Apple and R. F. Smith (eds.). *Integrated Pest Management*. New York, N.Y.: Plenum Press.

Soane, B.D. 1975. "Studies on some soil physical properties in relation to cultivation and traffic." In *Soil physical conditions and crop production*. MAFF Technical Bulletin 29, HMSO: London.

Sociedad Nacional de Agricultura (SNA). 1991. *Agronegocios*. Santiago: SNA.

Solazar-Rodriguez, J. I. 1985. Evaluación agronómica, ecologica y economica del sistema de agricultura organica en el cultivo de trigo como tecnologia alternative de produccion. Tesis Ing. Agronomo. Fac. De Agronomia. Univ. Catolica Valpariso, Quillota.

Stone, F. D. 1983. "Agricultural Changes as an Adaptive Process: Adoption of Modern Methods and Responses to Pest Outbreaks by Rice Farmers in Chachoengsao Province, Central Thailand." Ph.D. thesis, University of Hawaii, Honolulu.

Strong, D. R. 1980. "Biogeographic dynamics of insect-host plant communities." *Am. Rev. Entomol.*, Vol. 24:89–119.

Sumangil, J. P.; A. J. Dancel, and R. G. Davide. 1991. National IPM in the Philippines. A Country Report. Presented during a conference on Integrated Pest Management in the Asia-Pacific Region, 23–27 September 1991, Kuala Lumpur, Malaysia.

Tait, E. J. 1977. "A Method for Comparing Pesticide Usage Patterns Between Farmers." *Annals of Applied Biology* 86(3):229–240.

Tammen, Ronald L. Personal interview. July 27, 1990. Arlington, Virginia: Organic Foods Alliance.

Tans, P.P., I.F. Fung, and T. Takahashi. 1990. "Observational Constraints on the Global Atmosphere CO_2 Budget." *Science*, 247: 1431–8.

Taylor, C.R. and K.K. Frohberg. 1977. "The Welfare Effects of Erosion Controls, Banning Pesticides, and Limiting Fertilizer in the Corn Belt." *American Journal of Agricultural Economics*, Vol. 59: 25–36.

Teng, P. S. 1990. "Crop Loss Assessment: A Review of Representative Approaches and Current Technology." *In IRRI, Crop Loss Assessment in Rice*.

____.1990. "Integrated Pest Management in Rice: An Analysis of the Status Quo with Recommendations for Action." Report submitted to the International Integrated Pest Management Task Force. 86 pp.

____. 1989. "Integrated Pest Management in Rice: An Analysis of the Status Quo with Recommendations for Action." A report prepared for the International Integrated Pest Management Task Force (ACIAR/IDRC/FAO/ONNRI/USAID).

____. (ed.). 1987. *Crop Loss Assessment and Pest Management*. St. Paul, Minn.: American Phytopathological Society Press.

____. 1986. "Crop Loss Appraisal in the Tropics." *Journal of Plant Protection in the Tropics* 3(1):39–50.

Teng, P. S.; C. Q. Torres; F. L. Nuque, and S. B. Calvero. 1990. "Current Knowledge on Crop Losses in Tropical Rice." *In* IRRI, *Crop Loss Assessment in Rice.*

Tweeten L. and G. Helmers. 1990. "Comment on alternative agriculture systems." In *Alternative Agriculture: Scientist's Review*. Spec. Pub. No. 16, Council for Agricultural Science and Technology, Ames, Iowa.

U.S. Department of Agriculture. 1990. *1990 Farm Bill: Proposal of the Administration*. Washington, D.C.: Office of Publishing and Visual Communications, February 1990.

____. 1989. 1989 Agricultural Chartbook. Agriculture Handbook No. 684. Washington, D.C.: Economic Research Service.

____. 1980. Study Team on Organic Farming. *Report and Recommendations on Organic Farming*. Washington, D.C.: U.S. Department of Agriculture.

U.S. Department of Agriculture, Economic Research Service. 1993. *Agricultural Outlook*. April.

U.S. Embassy. 1990. "Chilean agriculture: integrating into world markets." *Sectoral Outlook Report*. May 1990. Santiago: U.S. Government.

U.S. General Accounting Office. 1990. *Alternative Agriculture: Federal Incentives and Farmers' Opinions*. GAO/PEMD-90-12. Washington, D.C.

U.S. House of Representatives. 1990. Food, Agriculture, Conservation, and Trade Act of 1990. Report 101-916. 101st Congress, 2d Session.

____. 1989. Sustainable Agricultural Adjustment Act of 1989, H.R. 3552. 101st Congress, 1st Session.

Waddell, Thomas E., ed. 1985. *The Off-Site Costs of Soil Erosion: Proceedings of a Symposium Held in May 1985*. Washington, D.C.: The Conservation Foundation.

Waibel, H. 1990. "Requirements for an Economic Interpretation of Crop Losses." *In* IRRI, *Crop Loss Assessment in Rice.*

____.1986. "The Economics of Integrated Pest Control in Irrigated Rice: A Case Study from the Philippines." *Crop Protection Monographs*. Berlin: Springer-Verlag.

Wali, A.M.O. El, F. LeGrand and G.J. Gascho. 1980. "Nitrogen leaching from soil and uptake by sugarcane from various urea based fertilisers." *Journal of Soil Science Society of America*, Vol. 44: 119–22.

Walker, D.J. and D.L. Young. 1986. "Assessing Soil Erosion Productivity Damage." In, *Soil Conservation: Assessing the National Resources Inventory*, Vol. II.: 21–62. Washington, D.C.: National Academy Press.

Walker, P. T. 1990. "Insect Pest-Loss Relationship: Characteristics and Importance." *In* IRRI, *Crop Loss Assessment in Rice.*

Walker, T. S., and K. V. Subba Rao. 1982. "Risk and the Choice of Cropping Systems: Hybrid Sorghum and Cotton in the Akola Region of Central Peninsular India." International Crops Research Institute for Semi-Arid Tropics, Economic Progress Report No. 43, Hyderabad, India.

Williams, J.R., et. al. 1989. *EPIC—Erosion/Productivity Impact Calculator: 2, User Manual*. Technical Bulletin No. 1768, A.N. Sharpley and J.R. Williams, eds. Washington, D.C.: U.S. Department of Agriculture.

____. 1981. "Soil erosion effects on soil productivity: A research perspective." *Journal of Soil and Water Conservation*, Vol. 36, No. 2: 82–90.

Williams, J.R. and K. G. Renard. 1985. "Assessments of Soil Erosion and Crop Productivity with Process Model (EPIC)." In *Soil Erosion and Crop Productivity*, ed. Follett and Stewart. Madison, Wisconsin: American Society of Agronomy.

Williams, J.R., P.T. Dyke, and C.A. Jones. 1982. "EPIC - A model for assessing the effects of erosion on soil productivity." Proceedings of the Third International Conference on State-of-the-art in Ecological Modelling. Fort Collins, Co.: Colorado State University.

Williams, R.J.B. 1978. "Effects of management and manuring on physical properties of some Rothamsted and Woburn soils." *Report of the Rothamsted Experimental Station for 1977, Part 2*.

Woodburn, Allan. 1990. "The Current Rice Agrochemicals Market." *In* B. T. Grayson, M. B. Greene, and L. G. Cropping (eds.), *Pest Management in Rice*. London and New York, N.Y.: Elsevier Applied Science.

Woods, Arthur, 1974. *Pest Control: A Survey*. New York, N.Y.: John Wiley and Sons.

World Commission on Environment and Development. 1987. *Our Common Future*. New Delhi: Oxford University Press.

World Health Organization (WHO). 1990. *Public Health Impact of Pesticides Used in Agriculture*. Geneva.

____. 1986. *Early Detection of Occupational Diseases*. Geneva.

Zandstra, I. 1987. "Lever-Operated Knapsack and Hand-Held Sprayers Used in Agriculture in Developing Countries: A Review of Their Safety and Efficacy." International Development Research Center, Ottawa, Canada.

____. 1976. "E.M.G. Voltage and Motor Nerve Conduction Velocity in Organophosphorous Pesticide Factory Workers." *International Archives of Occupational and Environmental Health* 36:267–74.

Zandstra, I., and I. E. Trollope. 1979. "Nerve Conduction Velocity and Refractory Period as Parameters of Neurotoxicity. *Electroencephalography and Clinical Neurophysiology* 46:351–54.

Zuñiga, E. 1985. "Ochenta años de control biologico en Chile. Revisión histórica y evaluación de los proyectos desarrollados (1903–1983)." *Agricultura Tecnica*, Vol. 45: 175–183.

World Resources Institute

The World Resources Institute (WRI) is a policy research center created in late 1982 to help governments, international organizations, and private business address a fundamental question: How can societies meet basic human needs and nurture economic growth without undermining the natural resources and environmental integrity on which life, economic vitality, and international security depend?

Two dominant concerns influence WRI's choice of projects and other activities:

The destructive effects of poor resource management on economic development and the alleviation of poverty in developing countries; and

The new generation of globally important environmental and resource problems that threaten the economic and environmental interests of the United States and other industrial countries and that have not been addressed with authority in their laws.

The Institute's current areas of policy research include tropical forests, biological diversity, sustainable agriculture, energy, climate change, atmospheric pollution, economic incentives for sustainable development, and resource and environmental information.

WRI's research is aimed at providing accurate information about global resources and population, identifying emerging issues, and developing politically and economically workable proposals.

In developing countries, WRI provides field services and technical program support for governments and non-governmental organizations trying to manage natural resources sustainably.

WRI's work is carried out by an interdisciplinary staff of scientists and experts augmented by a network of formal advisors, collaborators, and cooperating institutions in 50 countries.

WRI is funded by private foundations, United Nations and governmental agencies, corporations, and concerned individuals.